The Shock Doctrine
of the Left

Graham Jones

———

The Shock Doctrine
of the Left

polity

The right of Graham Jones to be identified as Author of this Work has been asserted in accordance with the UK Copyright, Designs and Patents Act 1988.

First published in 2018 by Polity Press

Polity Press
65 Bridge Street
Cambridge CB2 1UR, UK

Polity Press
101 Station Landing
Suite 300
Medford, MA 02155, USA

ISBN-13: 978-1-5095-2854-7 (hardback)
ISBN-13: 978-1-5095-2855-4 (paperback)

A catalogue record for this book is available from the British Library.

Library of Congress Cataloging-in-Publication Data

Names: Jones, Graham, 1985- author.
Title: The shock doctrine of the left / Graham Jones.
Description: Cambridge, UK ; Medford, MA : Polity Press, 2018. | Series: Radical futures | Includes bibliographical references and index.1
Identifiers: LCCN 2018000351 (print) | LCCN 2018018170 (ebook) | ISBN 9781509528585 (Epub) | ISBN 9781509528547 (hardback) | ISBN 9781509528554
   (pbk.)
Subjects: LCSH: Right and left (Political science) | Direct action. | Radicalism.
Classification: LCC JA83 (ebook) | LCC JA83 .J64 2018 (print) | DDC 320.53--dc23
LC record available at https://lccn.loc.gov/2018000351

Typeset in 11 on 15 Sabon by Servis Filmsetting Ltd, Stockport, Cheshire
Printed and bound in the UK by Clays Ltd, Elcograf S.p.A.

For further information on Polity, visit our website: politybooks.com

Contents

Figures

Preface

The world is a body. It grows in complexity
by the day. And it is sick.

The list of ailments is long: from climate change and
nuclear intimidation; resurgent fascism and the con-
stitutional mess of Brexit; stagnant economies and
the threat of mass technological unemployment;
to the increasing precarity of work, housing and
mental health. Without a system for making sense
of this chaos, many people are at a loss. We cannot
plan or predict our futures. We feel out of control.

'Take Back Control' the Brexit campaign said, and
it resonated. Without a coherent progressive framework for sifting through the complexity, people
grasp for whatever explanations they can find. What
could be the slogan of a radical democratic project
becomes one of isolation and border violence. This

book aims to contribute to an alternative vision which can help us to understand, act collectively within, and change the course of this chaos. It is part narrative, part toolkit, part manifesto.

There are too many to name who have contributed to this book, most of them unknowingly. Perhaps we cared for one another, picked each other up when we had no more strength. Perhaps we worked together to build a new world, in our organizing, our actions, our discussions or celebrations. Perhaps you made chaos in my life, or I made it in yours. Likewise, these are the core themes of the book: the necessity of care in reproducing our movements, the dynamics of creating counterpower, and how understanding chaos and complexity is key to all of this.

There are nonetheless certain people I must thank individually. My family, who created me, supported me, and have always been there for me. Nick Srnicek, Alex Williams and Helen Hester, who have been my best advocates within the academy. Harriet for giving me a place to stay in London along with loads of emotional support during the writing of this book. Roger and Joel from Radical Think Tank, who contributed significantly to the development of these ideas through our conversations, workshops and co-organizing. My Radical

Preface

Assembly friends, from whom I learned so much, and Brick Lane Debates, who set me on a path. Alex and Tammy for their ideas, encouragement and unconditional care in equal measure. David Bell for inspiring my first forays into theory. Everyone who has supported me on Patreon (Maro, Al, George, Het, Steffan, Destro), and those who have helped financially during my frequent crises; I owe my health to you. All of those who took part in and helped to organize the Revolution and Complex Systems course, particularly Shiri from Anti-University Now. Brendan for our inspiring conversations. Plan C comrades who have contributed to discussions and for generously hosting me to talk about them. Patra, for your emotional support during the most difficult times of my life; you are wonderful. Louise for teaching me how to care more. Ramzy for your encouragement to publish, after I did the same for you. Felix, Greygory and everyone at Open Barbers, for all your love and guidance. Bonnie and Nick for teaching me the essentials of organizing, and for the excellent cooking. The New Materialisms reading group for always making me feel welcome. Liam Barrington Bush for our productive debates and your inspiring activism. Lindsay for being an incredibly strong set of shoulders for me to cry on so many times. Isla for your kindness and pragmatism in equal measure. Sophie and Stef for keeping my spirits up with animal pictures at unexpected moments. Rosie and Joel for a quiet space to write and cats to play with. Frankie and Abi for being writing pals. Char for inspiring me to start writing many years ago. I have undoubtedly missed many who deserve their place. It is a privilege to have known so many great people that I struggle to count them all.

Introduction

I woke on the morning after the 2015 general election and headed straight to social media. A Conservative victory. The left-wing bubble was in shock; five years of disastrous austerity should have seen them off, or so we thought. Murmurs of hope were building around leftist projects elsewhere in Europe, such as Podemos in Spain and Syriza in Greece. But Britain's left populist moment was yet to come, future Labour leader Jeremy Corbyn still a relative unknown on the backbenches.

That weekend, the quiet at home felt jarring given the intensity of events, and I felt compelled to travel over to Whitehall where I heard people were assembling. Forty minutes later I was in the middle of a growing crowd of angry people. A police line had formed to hold us away from Downing Street. There was jostling, but no real violence. Until, that is, a line of police charged through the crowd, penning in the innermost protesters. All hell broke loose.

The crowd scattered, green smoke grenades were set off, batons were raised, projectiles were launched. Riot police arrived in waves. I had seen the tactic of 'kettling' before, trapping people for hours at a time before arrests, but I had not been in one, and feared that arrest could mean losing my job. Someone spotted that police were starting to block the road further down. The crowd fled, and I was swept along.

The panicked runners flocked down Whitehall, all turning in sync as they saw the path ahead blocked. We leaped over barriers onto a lawn and charged across, a thin line of officers grabbing randomly and wildly at the crowd that was breaking past. I felt impacts, but adrenaline was numbing any pain. I reached the opposite side and someone dragged me over the fence to safety. As we walked away, I noticed my heart pounding in my throat, and an ache in my upper arm started to swell.

Something changed in me at that moment. All I had wanted was not to be arrested for standing and watching a protest, and yet here I was bruised and panicking. Is that all it takes, I thought? I had done some organizing prior to this, mainly with housing groups, writing community newssheets and protesting outside the local housing association. But the energy in that moment awakened something – a realization of possibilities. Watching the crowd swarm and shift as one body, being carried away with it, having its unconditional support in taking me to safety. For a brief moment I felt part of something larger than myself.

The days that followed were a blur. A group of activists had seized the moment, calling an assembly to discuss what the left should do next, and I went along to their planning meeting to see if I could help. We met at a squat in Fitzrovia, an empty multi-storey office building, secured with a large improvised door bolt and newspaper-covered windows. A quiet anxiety and excitement rattled in the air with the sense of potential that had opened up, and perhaps also from knowing a police van was parked across the road keeping an eye on us. We sat on the carpeted floor, and as the meeting began I noticed something unfamiliar about the atmosphere: it was caring. Everyone was given space and encouraged to speak. There was a diversity of age, race, gender and class. The stressfulness of the situation was acknowledged. I was less afraid than usual for my odd behaviours and mental health issues to be on show. We shared food. Again, I had that feeling of being part of a larger body, albeit a safer sort.

Introduction

Less than a week later, in a large hall beneath the Institute of Education, the assembly was getting underway. A thousand people filed through the doors, filling the auditorium and spilling out around the edges. Banners were hung across the walls, the floor was quickly carpeted in discarded leaflets. Over a few hours of speeches, group discussions and votes, productive ideas as well as a great many tensions emerged. Some feared that starting another top-down organization would repeat the failures of the anti-austerity movement; others worried that a lack of leadership could see another Occupy-like mobilization that created no lasting institution. Some railed against leftist language which alienated the majority, while others feared that a lack of analysis of capitalism would lead to a movement that forever reproduced it. Some objected to the hostile location of a university building. Others were just thankful we had booked a wheelchair-accessible venue.

Nonetheless, by the end of the night we had planted the seeds of a new organization. People were arranged into groups based on location; they swapped details, and began to discuss how to start organizing locally. We began an attempt to create a new body, larger than ourselves. In time it would have both successes and failures, growths and declines, and would begin to resolve some of those tensions – while finding new questions in the process. These same tensions and questions underlie the explorations in this book.

Chaos

This period of chaos had many parts: electoral, insurrectionary, emotional and organizational. There were shocks on different scales, from the national to the individual – one cascading into the next. Energy eventually depleted, stability returned, and a new order emerged. Moments like this can come without warning, whether in a natural disaster, an economic shock, or a death. Others will occur on a date we can plan for: elections, referenda, or major cultural events. In each case, existing relations are upended: friendships, organizations, expectations, whole lives can fall apart and be remade, patterns of movement in our daily lives suddenly altered. The Olympic development reordering the layout of the city with new stadiums, roads and train stations; the terror attack changing routines and precautions. The old is swept aside, and the new rapidly takes its place. What this 'new' will be, however, remains to be seen.

Introduction

Chaos is not randomness – it is extreme sensitivity. Where there is disorder in a dynamic body – like a human body, a city, the earth's ecosystem – small changes can cause anything from no effect to earth-shatteringly large outcomes. Its future is still, however, determined by its past, but at a level of complexity that makes it impossible to predict.

We often think of chaos as a purely bad thing, and it certainly can be at certain times and places. The chaos unleashed by the election result led to injuries and traumas, but also to new experiences, new friendships, new organizations. Indeed, living bodies always exist on the *edge of chaos*, maintaining just enough stability while undergoing rapid change. It is truer to say that chaos is productive, whether what it produces is to our advantage or not.

Shock Doctrine

In *The Shock Doctrine*, Naomi Klein described how neoliberalism had come to power through manipulating chaos. Long before Thatcher and Reagan began to enact neoliberal policies, thinkers like Milton Friedman were seeding their ideas into networks of organizations. The vision of privatizing state assets, removing barriers to trade, and cutting public spending flowed through universities, the media, political parties and think tanks, over time moving from fringe theory to common sense. Those ideas were then ready to hand when existing social theories fell apart.

Whether deliberately causing chaos or preparing for it, right wingers learned to use these moments to their advantage. Any time the public was disorientated and normal social processes were disrupted became an opportunity for putting their ideas into practice. Terror attacks, natural disasters, civil wars and economic crashes have all been used to enact changes far beyond what would normally be possible.

Can anything coming out of this inform a left alternative? Clearly the policy content is opposed to our goals. But the form of the shock doctrine is another matter. We can embed our visions in a network of organizations; align the left around a preparation for shocks; and in those moments enact rapid, irreversible change. This broadest outline of a strategy would enable us to move beyond reactive mobilizations and towards an active collective project.

If the task involves aligning the left, however, we first need to address its divisions.

Introduction

Logics of the Left

Crowds fill the streets to confront an enemy, marching, occupying buildings, squaring up to police and fascists. Elsewhere, others quietly build functioning alternatives to the current system, through workers' cooperatives, social centres and community currencies. Online, people come together across wide areas demanding social justice for oppressed people, restructuring our movements away from domination by the white, the male, the able-bodied, the neurotypical, the heterosexual, the cisgender. Meanwhile leftist career politicians (very often white, male, able-bodied . . .) march through state institutions, aiming to change government policy through elections, lobbying and popular media. Each of these often finds itself at loggerheads with another. Some are criticized for their aggression, others for their isolation, some for their focus on differences without creation of new unity, and others for supporting the very systems we are often fighting against.

While these categories are fluid, and many will find themselves lying across their boundaries, they nonetheless reflect different broad emphases on how change happens. Do we focus on *smashing* our opponents, tearing apart their connections and allowing chaos to push us forward to a new society? Are we actively *building* an entirely new world today that we hope can take over tomorrow? Are we *healing* ourselves and our communities from oppression, marginalization and exploitation? Or are we *taming* those problems through incremental changes enacted by the state?

These four categories – Smashing, Building, Healing and Taming – will be used as lenses through which to examine how complex systems operate, while remaining relevant to political action. This typology was adapted from a work by sociologist Erik Olin Wright entitled *How to Be an Anticapitalist Today*. However, I have re-framed it to fit better within the model I shall set out in the next chapter, to the extent that they are now significantly different. Due to the dynamics explored later, I also reject some of his conclusions, such as his dismissal of smashing.

By examining the pros and cons of each category, we can extract observations about the dynamics of social movement. From this we can develop a strategic framework that incorporates these different logics, while mitigating their failures. This meta-strategy is what I call the Shock Doctrine of the Left.

Introduction

Accessible Complexity

Lenses need to be aimed at something. We need a model for understanding systems, one capable of bridging the levels that shocks operate on: physical, psychological, social and global. The key source I have drawn from is 'complex adaptive systems theory', a series of concepts used across various scientific disciplines. But this tends to be academic and impenetrable, whereas creating broad grassroots social movement requires accessibility. Efforts to translate these ideas into a popular idiom tend to destroy their usefulness, rendering them less as tools than as interesting facts. Rather than merely make these ideas more digestible, we need to re-mould them so that they are accessible for non-experts to take and apply.

Making radical ideas accessible means starting with what people already know. We place a wall in front of an audience if we ask them to think in cold, abstract terms like 'systems'. As explored later on in this work, language activates more than just definitions; it triggers emotions and networks of embodied knowledge. A word like 'system' links into such technical language as *process, error, diagram, logic, administrator*. In contrast, a word like 'body' will tend to trigger evocative and widely understood concepts like *human, naked, sex, heart, soul, death*. By using this more vivid, bodily language, we can make analyses more emotionally engaging.

I propose to use an overarching metaphor of *the body* for this reason. Our existing bodily experience will be used to introduce new concepts. Where possible, language is re-framed: 'systems' become bodies, 'trajectories' become paths that we walk down, 'bifurcations' become forks in that path, and so on.

The next chapter lays out the core of this model. Chapters 2 to 5 explore the dynamics of bodies in more detail through the four logics of the left. The final chapter combines these into a meta-strategy: the Shock Doctrine of the Left.

1

The Body Model

The Shape of Your Body

Let us start somewhere familiar: our own bodies. Focus on the feeling as you sit or stand or walk or lie. Scan downward from your head to the other extremes of your body. Feel the weight of your torso. The points of tension in your back. The taste in your mouth. The rise and fall of your chest with every breath.

Descend inwards, to what you cannot directly feel or control but know is there: bones and joints and muscles, a solid structure supporting lungs and heart and brain, directing blood and oxygen and nerve impulses, enabling thought and movement and keeping all the processes of your body flowing. This multitude of parts makes up the physical aspect of your body. These parts are neither isolated nor randomly arranged, but relate to each other in regular patterns.

Because of these patterns, your body is able to act in ways that its parts cannot. The whole human body can perform actions – whether thinking, eating, talking, typing, screaming – where neither the brain, limbs, bones nor blood could do this alone. We therefore have three core elements in the organization of a body: differentiated *parts*, which *interact* in a sustained pattern or structure, creating an *emergent whole* that is more than the sum of those parts.

This map of the body can be applied to all kinds of systems. Take the family. When I was young, our household included my mother, my father, my brother and myself: a set of parts. We interacted in a sustained pattern: my mother cleaning and cooking, my father paying the bills, fixing things and teaching music in the living room, both of them working during the week, the two children going to school and home again, sitting at the table for dinner and getting to bed on time. Through those interactions my parents were able to feed us, house us, have us educated, all four keeping each other feeling happy, loved and assured of a stable future. The family had emergent powers that no individual on their own possessed. If that organization ever broke down, then those emergent powers of safety and security could do likewise. In this way, a family is a body.

Now let us leave the immediate. Feel yourself becoming lighter. You begin to float, rising higher and higher, breaking through the clouds. You soar over a city, towers jutting up towards you, the smell of smog burning your nostrils. Looking down you see cars, trains and people passing through the veins of its streets, to the organs of its offices, shops and libraries. Unseen electrical wires act like synapses firing across the city. There are regular patterns of movement, flows waxing and waning by day and night, guided by the commute, by lunchtimes, and the weekend; by the papers, the post, the 10 o'clock news. Together these create a body which can sustain a populace, create jobs, build houses, keep people healthy, and more. It can equally fail to produce those powers, instead bringing poverty, pollution, sickness and unemployment. A city is a body.

We can even see the earth as a body, made up of its seas and lands and air, of biogeochemical cycles of gas and rock and water, producing a whole that makes life on the planet possible. And we make our mark on those cycles. The earth is criss-crossed with human activity, humans as much a part of the body as forests, oceans and glaciers. A massive network of cities and transport infrastructure drive rising temperature and sea levels, expanding deserts, ocean acidification and melting ice caps. The earth is a body, one we are part of and one that we are choking.

These different scales of body are nested. The human becomes part of a relationship, nested within a family, which is within a community, which is within a town or city, which is part of a global intercity network, which is part of the earth. In the same way, the human can become part of an organization, which is part of a local coalition, in a city-wide social movement, itself part of a national uprising, and a global revolution. A whole body can become a part of a larger body. This nesting of bodies-within-bodies-within-bodies allows us to picture the linkages between psychological, social and global organization.

This framework can help us to understand structures, but not change. For that, we must incorporate time.

The Path of Your Body

You are moving through your home. You feel the room with the senses available to you: its textures coarse and smooth, or sights dull and bright, or smells musty and sweet. You focus on an object, remembering the person who gave it to you. For a moment you live in the past, experiencing again that person, that place, their character. Back then you imagined a future, but of course the reality turned out to be quite different. Perhaps how these memories appear to you today is also quite different to how they felt at the time.

In every moment, you have a past, a present and a future. We experience a flow of sensation in the present moment, but it is understood through how our bodies have responded in the past, and how we hope to be in the future. The past lives on in our memories, in how we have learned to navigate our environments, in the habits we have created, in our knowledge, in the very shape of our bodies. Our pasts are embedded within us, like the rings and knots in a tree trunk, or the sag in an old chair where someone used to sit.

The future too lives in the present, in all the potentials alive within us. I can run, but I am not running now. I can swim, but likewise I remain sitting. These living potentials are not currently activated, but are still a real part of my body in this moment. They shape the futures that I can or am likely to experience. By finding new experiences in the present, I empower my body to control my path into the future.

To get a sense of how this can apply to wider social bodies, let us again visit that smog-filled city. You can trace the layers of the past in the changing architecture, new stacked atop old, in how the layout changes after wars or terror attacks or rapacious property development. You can see it in the ancient towns, their paths knotted and twisting, following the routes of the inhabitants as they carved out their worlds; quite unlike the gridlike rationality of the modern planned town. Economic crashes bringing skeletal high streets, shifting poverty and pain through generations. The ghost of the British Empire kept alive through its statues, its symbols, its heroes.

These pasts converge with those of other bodies in the present, defining a future path for the whole; to be an imperial centre, which sucks resources from the global periphery, or to be on the receiving end of this subjugation. To become prosperous, deprived or sharply divided. To shape itself in preparation for those futures, driving towards revolution or recoiling from civil war.

This model provides a simple but widely applicable tool for understanding complex bodies. Parts in relation creating emergent wholes. Past, present and future synthesized in every moment to produce change.

Rival Body Metaphors

Beyond making complex thought more accessible, the body metaphor links us back into the shock doctrine – and here we must take caution. As Naomi Klein points out, the architects of neoliberalism used the language of the 'social body' being 'contaminated with disease' (i.e. socialism), and that the violent repression and economic chaos they created was 'a natural reaction to a sick body'. Organic metaphors for society are also found in Nazi discourse and the medieval 'body politic', both of which sought to justify repression in the name of social stability. We therefore need to be extremely careful in evoking similar metaphors to avoid carrying across their implications. On the other hand, this provides a point at which we can struggle for alternative emancipatory understandings of this language. As Chapter 5 will show, it is important that we contest the meanings of language rather than allowing our opponents to control them. Further, the complexity of the model developed over the following chapters – including its focus on change, the future, and difference – will demonstrate itself as resistant to being used as a tool of Conservative or fascist domination, particularly in the emotional aspects explored in Chapter 4.

Every Body is an Organizer

The body model of 'parts–relations–wholes, pasts–presents–futures' can be used as a tool for engaging in social struggle. When planning action, mapping the parts and relations within our opponents can highlight their weaknesses and our potential allies. When building organizations, a focus on how parts are interacting can inform how we design and structure bodies to create the powers we want to emerge. In mediating interpersonal disputes, and unlearning and healing from oppressions, it can help to understand how bodies on divergent paths have created conflict, and to ensure that the needs of all bodies affected are taken into account, in all their differences of experience and knowledge. And in navigating the corridors of power, it can help us understand how and why our paths can be corrupted, and what we can do to prevent this.

One lesson the model can immediately provide for political organizing is this: everybody is an organizer. Or rather, every *body* is an organizer – of its parts, of the wholes it is part of, and of its environment. We organize our social bodies and they organize us. We are born into social bodies with histories that guide, constrain and empower us. Structures of oppression, poverty, neoliberal ideology, 'that is just the way things are'; all are the memory of bodies, of the clashes of the past, embedded in social and psychological structure. And yet it is we who reproduce this, in our individual and collective behaviour, in every moment. We create the present which will be the next generation's past, shaping the future for ourselves and for every generation to come.

Making people aware of this power, and equipping them with the skills to use it, should be the focus of the left. Understanding the pasts we have come from, knowing our available interventions in the present, with a vision of an empowered future. When someone makes themselves aware of all this, and begins to act to change the world around them, they become revolutionary.

Beyond the human individual's body, so too can any larger-scale body become revolutionary. An organization that is currently disconnected from social movements can become revolutionary, such as how churches formed the backbone of the civil rights movement. A whole city can become a revolutionary body, like the contemporary municipal movements in Spain, or a cross-country network of bodies like the Venezuelan system of communal councils. Ultimately, the Shock Doctrine of the Left calls to create revolutionary bodies at every scale, all the way up to the whole earth.

But first, we must descend back to ground level, and look more closely at the body through our four lenses.

Further Reading

The Systems View of Life by Fritjof Capra and Pier Luigi Luisi provides an overview of the complex systems concepts which underlie the rest of this book. *Political Affect* by John Protevi translates the ideas of Deleuze and Guattari into complex systems terms, using the similar concept of 'bodies politic' to analyse events like Hurricane Katrina and the Columbine massacre. *Process-Relational Philosophy* by Robert Mesle is an accessible introduction to Alfred North Whitehead, whose 'philosophy of organism' shares aspects of our body model – the notion of 'concrescence' for example reflects the synthesis of past, present and future.

The Body Model

Tektology: The Universal Organizational Science by Alexander Bogdanov was an early attempt (by a rival of Lenin's) to adapt Marxism towards a systems perspective similar to ours, and a precursor of today's complex systems theory. *The Entropy of Capitalism* by Robert Biel is in contrast one of the only sustained applications of complex systems ideas to contemporary Marxist analysis.

Interlude

The march was small, and security was light. Only one lane of traffic was taken up by the moving crowd, and the rest of the city went about its business. The police had clearly expected a gentle affair. You had other ideas.

You wait for the right moment. As the march turns a corner, the traffic lights go red, leaving a window of opportunity – you storm out into the road with a group, unfurling a huge banner extending across the intersection, blocking traffic from all directions. The rest of the march, instead of continuing on as expected, scatters and re-forms around the new blockade. A tailback quickly builds up, drivers honking their horns in irritation before becoming resigned to the wait. Chants ring out, the ones you had helped write and practise with other organizers the previous weekend. A sound system arrives and speeches begin. Individuals walk round to speak to people in cars, handing them leaflets to explain why they were taking the action. Journalists and photographers you had tipped off begin scribbling notes and taking pictures that will make it into the newspapers.

You held the crossing for about an hour before the police lost their patience. More backup arrived, and denser police lines closed in, their commands increasingly aggressive. You became penned in, and the police began trying to tear the banner from your hands. In the scuffle, people were grabbed and pulled behind the police line. The adrenaline slammed through you, and your composure evaporated – a feeling you did not recognize took control, snap decisions appeared without forethought.

The crowd started to thin out shortly after. Traffic was restarted, the banner was gone, and those less prepared for violence had left. Others moved on to do arrestee support at the police station. You needed to sit and calm down first, so you headed off for the planned debrief in a local pub.

2

Smashing

Any action that blocks or breaks apart the connections between parts of a body, to prevent it producing an emergent whole, I call Smashing. Workers on strike block the flow of production that is the lifeblood of a business. A 'distributed denial of service' attack (DDOS) disables a website by overloading it with traffic. Winning a fight with fascists and demoralizing them to the extent their organizations fall apart. Even an act that suddenly smashes apart people's expectations could count: an unexpected embarrassment of a prominent figure whether through releasing sensitive information or a pie thrown in the face, can harm their reputation and the social, political and economic links it sustains. This chapter focuses largely on 'direct action' but in terms of bodily change we are interested in the smashing of the relations between parts, whether material, social, psychological or digital.

Smashing is not limited to actions that benefit the left. It also includes those situations described by Naomi Klein: the bulldozing of Palestinian towns, rapid privatization of New Orleans schools, or mass torture of Chilean leftists. These shocks aim to create and harness chaos, whether in physical infrastructure, in public expectations, or in the bodies of activists, in order to destroy movements, communities and any hope of progressive change. Understanding smashing dynamics is therefore of benefit for both resisting these shock tactics and developing our own.

Order

Order and chaos are not a binary, but the ends of a scale. Imagine a couple. Both are very tidy and organized, and value order. However, one has a fixed sense of how things should be, accepts no deviation, makes no compromise. The other by contrast will always take circumstances into account before making a decision, will always try to work with the other on conflicts. Thus, order may be rigid, or contain some flexibility. Order is needed for the regular relations between parts that create empowered wholes; but too much can be stifling, shutting down the possibilities that an element of disorder can bring.

Alternatively, one might be more a fan of disorder. We can be messy, reject trends, enjoy coarse language and humour; but if there is too much chaos, life becomes extremely difficult. We need to wash plates eventually or we will run out of things to eat from. We need to take the bins out eventually or diseases will spread. And we need to talk in coherent sentences, remember to wear clothes when we leave the house and so on, or else we will struggle to communicate and risk alienating those around us. Chaos can be total, or with enough stability for some consistent patterns to form. We need chaos for the dynamic element that creates the life of an adaptive body; but if there is too much, nothing holds together, and everything is disempowered.

We see this balance in comparing hierarchical and horizontal organizing, say between a large revolutionary 'vanguard' party, and a small direct action group. The order of formal, regular organization is necessary to create long-term power; but where those structures are inflexible, as hierarchies tend to be, it stifles the potential of the movement. On the other hand, non-hierarchical organizing can be an incredibly dynamic, creative melting pot, which can react rapidly to emerging events. However, it can fall apart in an instant, leaving no lasting trace. Both ends of the spectrum lead to disempowerment. Seeing hierarchical and horizontal less as a binary and more on a scale of order helps us to focus on those sweet spots in between that are the most effective.

Forks in the Road

She squared up to the fascist, a foot taller than her but shrinking by the second. We hadn't planned to end the night with a brawl; the thirty or so of us gathered at a pub in south London were there just to say goodbye to some friends leaving the city. But it was also forty years to the day since the Battle of Lewisham, and only twenty-four hours since the Unite the Right march in Charlottesville had brought the death of Heather Heyer. This fascist had chosen the wrong evening to preach publicly about the superiority of the white race.

The night had been mostly cheerful but, as we sat among the tables outside, the bouncer began to set us on edge, singling out black and transgender people for harassment. A short while later a crowd swelled around the front of the pub. A bald, burly man had joined the bouncer and both began facing down a much smaller but defiant woman. We came to a fork in the road, a standoff, where multiple different futures came into view: Will a fight break out? Will he leave? Will we?

We encounter forks in the road all the time, of greater or lesser significance. The decision to make myself a tea rather than a coffee is a fork of sorts, but one unlikely to change any larger path. More significant forks in our lives are deciding which school to attend, whether to take a new job, where we should move to, whether or not to have children. These can significantly alter our path, in some cases creating whole new bodies with their own paths: a new child, a new family, a new network of friends. And some forks have global resonance. The decision in 2011 of Mohammed Bouazizi to set himself alight triggered a wave of protests across North Africa and the Middle East. The assassination of Archduke Franz Ferdinand precipitated a world war. What happens in these decisive moments these *bifurcations* – is that small decisions, instead of leading to a small change, can lead to huge changes in a path. This 'sensitive dependence on initial conditions' is popularly known as the butterfly effect, a key aspect of chaotic dynamics.

Smashing

Although the outcome of a chaotic moment is unpredictable, it can still be influenced. When a shock occurs and our expectations fall apart, we scramble towards whatever alternatives are already lying around. The neoliberal project of embedding their ideas in an ecology of organizations meant that, at the moment of crisis, the initial conditions were already set in their favour, ready to guide events. The landscape around us limits our path, but equally it can be shaped in advance.

This preparation applies to social and physical infrastructure as well. In Egypt during the Arab Spring, the removal of Mubarak caused a period of chaos in which established actors like the military and the Muslim Brotherhood were able to take control. There was no other civil society body powerful enough to do so, like a formal coalition between trade unions and the youth that led the uprising. Compare this to the Russian revolutions of 1917. A network of Soviets – workers' councils – was already established prior to the October insurrection, providing an infrastructural vehicle which could take over governance. This body-of-bodies was therefore one of the 'initial conditions' which the chaos of the revolution could quickly realign around.

The desire for order has powerful influence, even

in spite of the content of that order. Positions which are usually pushed to the edges of public discourse become more palatable, if they provide a promise of restoring order. It is clear then why, with the collapse of the neoliberal order, we have seen such growth in the poles of both socialism and fascism. Shock in other words forces people to 'get off the fence', and this can increase public support for our movement, if we have prepared the ground.

We have little control over when many such shocks will occur. To create an active and not simply reactive strategy therefore, we need to be able to plan our own chaos.

Metabolism

The 'Stop the War' movement against the invasion of Iraq brought millions of people onto the streets. It included the largest protest in British history, and walkouts in schools, universities and workplaces. So why did it fail in its ultimate goal?

In his book Rebel Cities, David Harvey argues that the key to successful mass action is found in disrupting urban processes, as witnessed in the effectiveness of transport and logistics strikes:

Smashing

Thousands of delivery trucks clog the streets of New York City every day. Organized, those workers would have the power to strangle the *metabolism* of the city. Strikes of transport workers (as, for example, in France over the last twenty years, and now in Shanghai) are extremely effective political weapons. The Bus Riders Union in Los Angeles, and the organization of taxi drivers in New York and LA, are examples of organizing across these dimensions. When the rebellious population of El Alto [in Bolivia] cut the main supply lines into La Paz, forcing the bourgeoisie to live on scraps, they soon gained their political objective. It is in fact in the cities that the wealthy classes are most vulnerable, not necessarily as persons but in terms of the value of the assets they control. It is for this reason that the capitalist state is gearing up for militarized urban struggles as the front line of class struggle in years to come. (emphasis mine)

As the word *metabolism* suggests, a city survives through all the flows into, out of and within its body. Likewise, we survive because of the flows through our bodies. Food, water and oxygen goes in, various waste products come out. Blood flows round and round, delivering and replenishing. If a flow is affected you may become disempowered in some way: the body weakened, aching, diseased, suffocating. Eventually you may die. Your life *is* those loops, the cyclical paths within your body. Whether it is a human being or a city, bodies collapse if the flows that sustain them are blocked.

To threaten an opponent to the point of achieving large concessions, you have to disrupt the flows that sustain it. Union organizer Jane McAlevey shows in her book *No Shortcuts* how those unions that take regular militant worker-led strike action to disrupt businesses get far more transformative results than those focused on closed-door negotiations. The workers are the parts of the workplace body that maintain it through their interactions, so a collective stoppage effectively kills the business.

It is not only industrial production that can be smashed. A university relies on the smooth running of open days to ensure a flow of new students. In a six-week campaign calling for divestment from fossil fuels, King's Climate Action used these moments to organize high publicity mockery and defacement actions, culminating in a hunger strike by a PhD student. Through the threat of increasingly damaging publicity, the campaign achieved more of their demands in those few weeks than the formal negotiations had in years. Mockery can be a powerful tool, but too often it remains merely symbolic – such as the liberal US comedians who failed to harm the rise of Donald Trump. But if it actively harms the reproduction of the body, it can be extremely powerful. Effective disruptive action requires mapping the parts and relations that sustain a body, and identifying targets for blockage.

Returning to 'Stop the War', action that directly targeted the metabolism of the state war-machine was minimal and ad hoc, the movement's leadership largely not supporting escalation. The strategy seemed to be to put pressure on the government through the sheer weight of public opinion. This can work, as politicians need popularity to win elections and keep their jobs. But in this case, it was clear when the war began, one month after the historic protest, that this strategy had failed. Alternative points of leverage would have needed to be found. Walkouts were symbolically powerful but did not cause enough disruption to the metabolism of war; sabotages in weapons factories, occupations of arms dealers, and blockades of ports might have been a different matter.

Vital Organs

Certain parts of a body will often support far more relations than others. The heart and brain play a far more central role in the emergence of our whole body than one of our fingers. So, attacking the former is more likely to result in death or serious harm than attacking the latter.

It is the same within a transport network. If you were to blockade a station at the end of a line, such as Walthamstow Central on the London Underground, you would cause delays to that station and at least a small part of that line. But if you successfully blockaded Oxford Circus, right in the centre of the network, it would have knock-on effects for many different stations. A few simultaneous blockages could cause disruption across the entire city. It is for this reason that activists are becoming increasingly interested in transport and logistics, as areas such as shipping ports are vital organs mediating flows of capital across the globe.

This is why direct action should always follow a power analysis of the situation, identifying who or what are the most significant actors or parts of the bodies we are targeting. Hubs that see the greatest flows of communication, materials and so on, will often produce the largest effect for the smallest intervention, and so are the best targets for efficiently collapsing a body.

Vital organs are a weakness in ourselves as well. The loss of a prominent activist can be a blow to an organization, if their knowledge and connections were not passed on. In order to create a strong movement that can withstand such a shock, those who find themselves in central positions or with accumulations of knowledge need to distribute those powers.

That does not, however, necessarily imply 'leaderless movements', or the smashing of any instance of social power. The inverse is a far more powerful route: that of *leader-full* movements. We shouldn't discourage organic leaders in order to have equality in disempowerment; we should go out of our way to empower those who are less naturally inclined to leadership, or more marginalized, and move towards equality in empowerment – decentralization not through destroying our own nodes of power but by massively proliferating them.

Absorb and Accelerate

While causing a shock may accelerate certain processes, in most cases this mobilization will quickly fade away. If, however, we can absorb that released energy and feed it back into creating further shock, then we have a consistent engine, which I call an *accelerator*.

The concept of acceleration has received wider

attention on the left since the release of the Accelerationist Manifesto, which advocates harnessing the creative destructive power of technology made possible by capitalism, for anti-capitalist purposes. If the Shock Doctrine of the Left strategy is a form of 'accelerationism', it is a broader one, if potentially compatible. It involves mapping the bodies around us – their parts, relations and wholes, their paths and speeds – and developing interventions for altering them to our advantage. This allows us to expand 'acceleration' from a state-focused strategy (e.g. investing in technology), to one in which interventions can be made in bodies at any scale. Such analyses could also lead us to *slow* certain processes, or to accelerate not their growth but their collapse.

At the level of social movement, we can create an accelerator, beginning when people are mobilized either by our deliberate actions or by an unexpected social shock. If those people can be absorbed into organizing, it increases our capacity for direct action. Larger actions lead to larger mobilization, to larger organizational growth, and so on. These virtuous or vicious circles of amplification are often known as positive feedback. (Even where it is collapse that is amplified, it is still 'positive'.) The key to this cycle, the absorption, is what is usually missing on the left: systematic training.

Training empowers us by forming new order within the human body. New and existing parts – ideas, skills, interests – are combined to create new whole abilities, new powers – how to organize a strike, or a public assembly, or build a local campaign. People often do not get more involved in organizing because they feel they do not have the abilities, or the knowledge, or do not know where to start or are nervous they will be shunned. If, following a shock, we are able to guide people towards friendly, accessible and holistic training, providing them with all the basic tools they need to keep organizing, then we stand a better chance of getting more sustainable results from waves of mobilization.

As it stands, the left in Britain likes to focus on marches ending with long rallies, before going home. These are not necessarily useless, but alone they are. If these mobilizations were used to draw people into workshops teaching them new skills of self-organization and direct action, forming new organizations on the spot, this momentary empowerment could be made to last. Big central London marches could be the engine to accelerate swarms of action across the country.

Taken as a whole, this chapter suggests a starting point for countering the neoliberal shock doctrine:

using disruptive actions to create our own chaos, as the initial spark of an accelerator of movement growth, to feed larger and larger shocks. In order to grasp these moments fully, we will also need organizations ready to create and push for something new, and not merely destroy the old. This is therefore the focus of the next chapter.

Further Reading

This is an Uprising by Mark and Paul Engler demonstrates how polarizing direct action can build broad movements. *Linked: The New Science of Networks* by Albert-László Barabási explains concepts such as clusters and hubs (our 'vital organs'). *Organization of the Organizationless* by Rodrigo Nunes applies network concepts to theorizing contemporary social movements. *Dynamics of Contention* by Tilly, McAdam and Tarrow highlights features that reoccur across many different social movements. *Sisters Uncut's Action Toolkit* (available at http://www.sistersuncut.org) and *The Student Organizer's Handbook* (available at http://studenthandbook.ourproject.org) are great resources for those wanting to organize action themselves.

Interlude

You awake with a jump – this is your stop. Another journey to an unfamiliar part of the city, the fourth meeting of the week. Showing your face, making connections, refreshing emotional bonds, sharing ideas, building coalitions. The meeting passes in a blur of names and agenda items and action points and announcements and suddenly you are travelling again; no time to waste when there's another meeting to get to. The big formal meeting in the big fancy trade-union building, or packed into the corner of an old pub in Stratford, in the offices beneath the Battle of Cable Street mural, or a squat on posh Kensington High Street, a social centre with a trash-strewn garden, a beautiful community farm near Heathrow airport, a small dark basement cinema, a gathering in an airy flat high up in a Battersea tower block. You plot them all on a map and share

*it around as though to say 'Look at all this activity!
This is the revolution! What are you waiting for?!'*

*Next, a housing cooperative in Islington. You
were late but the meeting hadn't started yet. Your
mind was still racing with the world outside as
you got seated and took off your coat. Warmth
radiated from the cooking at the other end of the
room, to the long table where you sat, a beautiful
old table strewn with pots and pans and plates of
bread. You looked around you at the rustic décor,
forgetting for a moment you were in the city. The
residents talked animatedly about their situation,
being threatened with eviction, the land value now
high enough for the council to have made alternative plans for it. Other residents filtered in and out,
greeting us and leaving again. A loving, supportive
community, people of all different ages, races and
class backgrounds supporting one another, cooking
together, even hosting film screenings in this beautiful building.*

*It was a model for how housing could be. But
it was battling against the path of change in the
opposite direction, one that drags us towards isolation, atomization, individualism, and private profit.
It can be easy to forget in the whir of organizing,
in the abstractions of the left, the real things that
people fight for. Not just 'housing', but this house,*

Interlude

this home, this family, this feeling. A steaming bowl of stew is placed in front of you with a smile. You make a mental note to carry this moment with you on the hectic ride to the next meeting.

3

Building

Acts of smashing, while vital for disruption, do not create the kind of resilient, large-scale, long-term bodies needed to replace dominant powers. As we have seen, the direction our world takes in moments of chaos will be defined by the ideas and institutions that are already available. If we want a world of workplaces owned and run cooperatively, of political decision-making power in local community hands, we stand a much better chance if this is already being built in time for social shocks.

The creation and growth of alternatives to the current system I will file under *Building*. This can involve bringing together existing but separate groups (such as in a coalition), or establishing entirely new ones (such as starting a workers' cooperative). And it means building not just organizations that resist the world today, but ones that actively create the world we want to see.

Existing alternatives are often slow to grow, and pose little threat to much faster growing businesses. In trying to survive they may avoid integrating in capitalist markets, but in the process become isolated and insular. On the other hand they may try to compete, and risk becoming gradually subsumed into the capitalist system rather than genuinely challenging it. To tackle this, we need to examine why bodies fail to grow, or do so in undesirable directions.

Decay

The meeting had arrived at a familiar topic: we were running out of money. The collectively run social centre was a vital resource for a wide range of people, from sex workers' rights groups, grassroots cleaners' unions, language classes, community massage, and feminist and anti-racist groups. Most were voluntary and operated on little or no income, or even at a loss. A grant that had covered a chunk of the rent was coming to an end, and no sustainable alternative had been found. Not only that, but attendance at admin meetings was falling. It was no surprise, given that these were often tedious events, but they were essential to keep the place running. A solution had to be found.

These are common problems in revolutionary organizing. The demands of having to operate within a capitalist system (the very thing they are fighting against) makes it difficult to sustain and to grow. But while you may not be able to stop the tendency to decay – money and energy will always deplete over time – you can find ways to counteract it.

As they interact, all bodies decay – their 'entropy' increases. Think of a sandcastle: its shape represents one possibility out of billions of alternative positions of all those grains of sand. Any time any of those grains is disturbed – by the wind, by the vibrations of someone moving around it – a grain is far more likely to shift into one of those billions of alternative positions than any sandcastle position.

Likewise, because we live in (and are) constantly moving systems, our bodies tend towards breakdown over time. This is why we need to eat, drink and breathe. Like the hand needed to rebuild the sandcastle, we must constantly rebuild our bodies to stay alive. As your body tissue decays, you need to digest food to supply proteins to rebuild those cells. As money, energy and enthusiasm depletes, the social centre must also somehow replenish these resources. New inputs are constantly needed.

As new inputs replenish order, the disorder is passed from the body into its environment. Just as food becomes disordered in the process of digestion and is expelled as waste, the decay in the social centre is transferred into the bodies of the organizers: energy, enthusiasm, time and money become fatigue, frustration, bloated calendars and empty pockets. If this entropy is not similarly expelled, the body will break down

Recycling rubbish or using manure as fertilizer demonstrates this breakdown. Burying waste does not get rid of it, and over time poisons the environment to an extent that disrupts emergent powers (such as being able to support life), creating cascading failures into other bodies that rely on it. Recycling allows waste to contribute again to social and biological metabolisms. Entropy is never ending; it is merely passed from one body to the next.

Similarly, those stressed and 'broke' organizers can look for emotional and financial support from partners and friends, and work to get more money, so pushing the disorder into another sphere. If work remains unevenly distributed, however, one person can end up being the entropy sink for the whole body. Always picking up the slack, being the one who dips into their pockets, who sorts out disputes – they can become overloaded, mentally collapse, and drop out. And as they were a vital organ, this can have fatal consequences for the organization.

To make this sustainable we need an accelerator: one body empowering another and another; eventually returning to empower the first. What is being accelerated in this instance are the flows into and out of various bodies that replenish their powers. We need collective awareness of the need to care for each other, to be emotionally responsive, to share tasks and check in with people. To make accessible points of entry so new people feel comfortable coming along, to make spaces welcoming so people want to come back. To actively empower others so that they can become equal contributors to the resilience of the body.

On financial sustainability, one method practised by organizations like trade unions is membership dues, where a regular small sum is paid by each member each month. Sliding scales can be introduced based on income, although many smaller radical organizations still feel uncomfortable with the gatekeeping aspect. Another method is creating magazines or newspapers for sale. Both can, however, create perverse incentives, whereby an organization that survives by its ability to recruit and sell ends up concentrating its efforts on self-promotion, rather than more useful work in wider movement building.

Alternatively, the metabolism of radical groups could be supported through wider 'solidarity economies', where groups of workers' cooperatives, unions, urban farms and social centres actively support one another to meet each other's basic needs. Autonomous funding bodies (like Edge Fund and Solid Fund in the UK) could play a key part in this, crowdfunding donations from wider afield and distributing them across the solidarity economy to boost growth. The Catalan Integral Cooperative is one successful example, an anti-capitalist cooperative network, founded in 2010 and then hugely boosted by the catalyst of the Spanish 15M movement.

As it stands, such a body did not exist in the UK at the time of our social centre's meeting, so this has to be a goal for the future. We decided to remain on the lookout for funding from a range of sources, from grants, regular public donations and through fundraising events. But, like a pig sniffing for truffles, to uncover those resources in the environment would require sharp enough senses to find them.

Building

Sense and Response

Our senses are key to survival. It is how we find the resources we need, how we identify threats and communicate with others. Senses are what give us information about our present environment, which activate our existing knowledge built up through the past, and reorganize our bodies to bring about a desired future. If our senses are impaired, this can harm our ability to adapt and survive.

An organization senses. Take, for example, anarchist and syndicalist federations, which have for a long time used forms of direct democracy on national and international scales. At their best, these highly ordered structures enable groups to align their processes across vast distances, to allocate resources to where they are most needed, and give greater reach to recruitment and propaganda. And, by allowing all members to be involved in decision making and action, they can create a real sense of democratic empowerment.

But speed can be a problem. For changes to pass on an international level can mean requiring agreement at local, regional, national and international levels. This can mean months for even relatively uncontroversial proposals, or much more where there is need for discussion, re-drafting and various checks and balances.

What this structure provides in long-term stability therefore, it loses in ability to react quickly to global events as a unified force. A local branch may be able to mobilize rapidly for local issues, but this becomes more challenging at a national level, and more so across borders. Large organizations can become relatively isolated and inwardly focused. There are, in other words, potential whole-body powers that are not emerging.

By increasing the speed of the sensing process from input to response, we can improve an organization's ability to mobilize rapidly, to draw in resources to enable growth, and so strengthen their overall resilience. This could involve adding or removing structure (order) in different parts of the body, culling redundant rules and processes to allow more flexibility, or clarifying mechanisms for fast-track decisions. What is important is that changes do not compromise existing emergent powers, but amplify them.

Speed is important, not merely in our present organizing, but in terms of utopian visions. Similar structures of nested direct democracy have been proposed and experimented with as general systems of social organization, by thinkers and movements such as Murray Bookchin, the Rojavan Revolution,

Participatory Economics (Parecon) and radical municipalism. Formal international social bodies are indeed needed to coordinate around global issues. But without speed, and therefore the ability to respond rapidly to emergencies, whether man-made or natural, these would not have the resilience necessary to survive in a world of global communications, climate unpredictability, conflict or sabotage.

Speed does come with risks, however – of losing control and careering off the initial path. How do we ensure that as a body adapts, it avoids changing into something unrecognizable?

DNA

As we develop through life, dramatic changes occur to our bodies. In most cases these stay within fairly limited bounds: most people do not grow to be twenty feet tall, with six arms or green skin. Likewise, if we have children, we tend to produce a body that is recognizable as having come from us ('they have your eyes!'). This constraining effect is thanks to a code embedded within us, containing information needed to reproduce our bodies accurately, as well as being the initial conditions for the creation of any new body. In the human body, this is DNA.

Although other forms of dynamic body such as cities do not have a literal DNA, they can contain similar coding that allows bodies to maintain integrity as they grow and reproduce. Think of the formal rules, roles, policies and procedures that create boundaries for an organization. On larger scales, law and regulation function as a coding of the nation state, allowing it to be formally reproduced through its constant enactment by state institutions.

But organizational coding requires something more if it is to have the properties of human DNA. States and many organizations are centralized entities, which control their parts very rigidly. Humans do not reproduce in that way. Once I have children, although I may have certain legal rights to control them, they are nonetheless autonomous beings. Their bodies and their character will develop as a result of *their* experiences, not of mine. Eventually, they will grow into adulthood, and have as much or as little power as I do. Human reproduction is therefore neither rigid and factory-like, nor chaotic and producing utterly incompatible bodies, but is better described as 'guided self-organization'. You create a body which can develop however it wants;

but by setting very specific initial conditions you ensure it remains within certain boundaries.

Applying this to social movement is the key to getting the best of both hierarchical and horizontal organizational forms. To move from general coding to a DNA capable of guided self-organization, we need three things. Firstly, the written *code* must be accurate, showing how the organization truly functions, rather than an idealized version, and without missing any parts that you want to pass on, parts that are not often written down (such as informal aspects of the culture). Secondly, there must be a reliable and active means of *replication*, for example through induction and training, rather than relying on people picking up details as they go along. Thirdly, there must be a *catalyst* for reproduction, to make people realize that they want to take part.

(1) *Code*

The DNA of a social movement organization can be broken down into Story, Strategy and Structure. Story is the situation that the group is fighting against and what it is fighting for. Strategy is what concrete interventions the organization will take to bring about that vision. And Structure details the formal aspects of the organization that people need in order to participate – agreed principles, membership rules, democratic processes and so on. These core elements must be clear, memorable and accessible. It is essentially another way of mapping bodies: the relations between people within an organization, the relations between organizations in a social movement, and the relations between a movement and the broader social context.

In contrast to this detailed DNA, Occupy was incredibly simple: a name, a tactic of occupying public squares, and the 'We Are the 99%' identity. This allowed it to spread rapidly and virally, and for it to adapt to varying geographical and social contexts. But it also meant that there was little to stabilize the different groups around, no shared goal or long-term strategy. Camps developed in incompatible directions, some liberal and pro-electoral, others radical and favouring militant direct action. Fractures within camps make synchronization between camps in various locations more difficult, and prevent a lasting global institution from forming.

(2) *Replication*
We can replicate organizational DNA through induction and training events, in which we lay out everything someone needs to know to start work immediately. Face-to-face training is far more pow-

erful than a 'contact us to start a group' page on a website, more so even than a well-written 'how-to' manual. Another human directly giving someone these tools and the encouragement to use them creates a much greater sense of ownership and empowerment. Yet, because the DNA is relatively stable, any autonomous action that results can remain consistent with the wider body.

If, however, only a handful of people are training new recruits, growth will always be limited by the capacity of those trainers. In order to scale therefore, the accelerator needs one more aspect: *training new trainers*. If the holistic training shows people not just how to get started as organizers, but how to emulate the very training itself in their own communities or workplaces, then we have the possibility of a kind of viral growth.

If we set up a training event, though, why would anyone come?

(3) *Catalyst*
Whether a shock emerges organically or deliberately, the released energy and attention can catalyse the growth process. If we organize some public direct action to bring exposure to an issue, those whose attention is grabbed should be directed to an event local to them. If we are aware of upcoming

disruptions like an election, we should likewise be prepared. We could even be ready to react at short notice when unexpected chaos erupts. The group Radical Think Tank has in the past operated in such a way, which we ironically nicknamed COBRA, after the government's own emergency response committee. This involved being prepared to set up events and workshops at short notice to make use of emerging catalysts. The goal was not to bring people into an existing organization, but to help guide people's self-organization towards more effective methods (through facilitation training, direct action workshops and so on).

Some may understandably be wary of this shock orientation, given how existing organizations often seem to be 'ambulance chasing' to find new members. There is an important difference, however, because this is not necessarily 'join my organization, buy my paper, sign my petition, me me me'. It is about disseminating skills that enable people to take action on their own terms, whether or not they do so within your organization. We could be bringing people into workshops on how to start whole new organizations, through DNA designing days. Shocks can be as motivating for people to start a cooperative, as they can to get involved in direct action, if persuasive reasons can be shown, and if it is made as accessible as possible. One could even hold events that simply introduce people to the best existing campaigns in the area, with members on hand to get them involved. The goal ultimately is to ensure that people are absorbed into long-term autonomous organizing, not to favour one organization over another.

Focusing on how we contribute to a wider social movement (rather than parasitically favouring our own organization) means going beyond just growing our own bodies or creating new ones. We need to consider how we link with existing groups, and work together to form more powerful wholes.

Body Builders

It was an otherwise gentle and forgettable march through London, calling for 'more jobs'. But that was not really our style, being more inclined towards Fully Automated Luxury Communism than we were full employment. Instead, inspired by Srnicek and Williams' *Inventing the Future*, we organized a cheekily titled 'No Jobs' radical bloc, using the opportunity to promote a discussion around automation, basic income, lowering the working week, and care.

The bloc did not disrupt much, aside from perhaps

the expectations of other marchers and onlookers, with our purple smoke and face masks. On the day we had fun, dancing to pop songs with colourful banners. Pictures went viral, we got some coverage in national news, and sparked conversation on the issues. But, important as these carnival moments are, that was only part of the purpose. It created a focal point which we could orient around, opening up a variety of options for network building both before and after the day. In the weeks prior we organized events across the city, including participatory discussions on the demands, workshops on creating utopian visions, knowing your rights at protests, direct action, and banner-making sessions. We canvassed for support from other groups – domestic violence campaigners, basic income advocates, grassroots unions – and made efforts to connect people between them. And we used some of the subsequent publicity to draw people to training events, where we shared widely applicable skills of campaign building and self-organization. These peripheral actions are what build capacity, both of an organization and a wider social movement. A march is just the focal point that you can organize around, and not the goal itself.

If, as we have said, power emerges from the interaction of parts to form whole bodies, it follows that the most powerful revolutionary role is not that of the Molotov thrower or the speech-maker: it is the person who builds networks. The network theorist Manuel Castells refers to this as the 'network switcher' but, in the language of this book, we could equally call this the body builder. Either way, bringing new people into political organizing, forming coalitions between groups who do not yet interact, bridging gaps between segregated communities, mapping existing groups for others to discover: these form the backbone that supports social movement. The simple act of bringing a new group of people into a room, getting them to talk to one another, swapping details and starting to form long-term relationships – this allows organizing to continue even once you remove yourself from the picture. The emotional labour of creating bonds is the glue which builds a revolutionary movement.

Our growth cannot simply be an incremental one, however, bringing the edges of our networks to the centre. We must also break out of 'the bubble' itself, that is, more into social bodies which we currently have no connection to whatsoever. We cannot simply rely on mobilizing people via mailing lists of existing supporters, or through social-media posts targeted at people already engaging with us. We need to be building bodies that stretch into communities and workplaces which we are currently distant from.

Those highly connected vital organs that can be a vulnerability also allow you to spread quickly into new networks. In order to make the most of this, you need to consider the current 'structural holes' in the network around you. Supposing, for example, you find a person on social media who has a lot of connections, but none or only a few are mutual friends of yours. They are a vital organ in a community which you are cut off from. Extending into their networks, then, will open up a huge swathe of new contacts. A different person may have a far higher number of friends; however, if they are mostly already people you know, connecting with them is unlikely to open up new areas of the network. This observation – the 'strength of weak ties' – can help us to build beyond the bubble and connect to potential allies we are not yet reaching.

The same goes for offline: if you can find a way into a community in which you know no one, via a body central to that community, you can rapidly expand into uncharted territory. This is seen in the classic union organizing tactic of finding the 'organic leaders' in a workplace. These are often *not* those most radical or enthusiastic to organize, but rather those most looked up to by their fellow workers, and linked to strong networks of unmobilized people in the wider community. Once again, mapping all the relevant bodies is the way to uncovering these vital organs.

For the institutions of our shock doctrine to beat the neoliberal model, our organizational resilience must improve. The speed and distance of our sensing has increased massively with the internet and social media, but our opponents are still ahead, and getting faster. More activists and groups need to take on the role of body-builders, expanding the active left into new areas beyond the bubble, and constructing solidarity economies that can support the rest of the movement. Yet this new world we are building in the shell of the old – as the Industrial Workers of the World slogan goes – cannot merely be a world of more effective organizations. We must also revolutionize the quality of interpersonal relations, healing the scars of oppressive pasts. The next chapter therefore looks at creating bodies that are diverse, accessible and liberatory.

Building

Further Reading

Elinor Ostrom's Rules for Radicals: Cooperative Alternatives Beyond Markets and States by Derek Wall is an accessible introduction to the leading theorist of managing common resources. *No Shortcuts: Organizing for Power in the New Gilded Age* by Jane McAlevey contains invaluable lessons on creating long-term grassroots power. *Seeds for Change* (https://www.seedsforchange.org.uk/resources) provides practical resources for building organizations. *Communication Power* by Manuel Castells is the source of the 'network switcher' (or 'body-builder') concept, and also contains insights about cognition and changing public opinion. *Omnia Sunt Communia: On the Commons and the Transformation to Postcapitalism* by Massimo De Angelis applies systems-theory concepts such as 'autopoietic systems' (our sensing bodies) to building an alternative to capitalism.

Interlude

Midwinter. People trickled back in, smelling of ciga-
rettes. A circle of chairs was formed, others making
tea or wandering about nervously before being
seated. When eventually everyone had returned, the
support group reconvened. You sat, body heavy,
avoiding eye contact, listening. Stories of depres-
sion, of schizophrenia, of autism, of hospitalization,
of the grind of work and the grind of poverty. Of
the drip drip drip of sexism, racism and ableism. Of
life under capitalism.

It came your turn to speak, but all you could
manage was a croaked apology. The chair gave a
warm smile and assured everyone it was ok if they
did not feel like speaking. As the meeting progressed,
the heaviness of the room gradually seemed to lift.
Eyes began to meet, bodies straightened, voices
got louder. As the room lifted you felt yourself lift

too. As it once again came your turn to speak, you spoke – this time clearly – and the bodies around you seemed to ease further. By the end of the session, the room was animated, with even the quieter people chipping in and laughing along.

Most days, it is hard not to feel isolated. Doctors and therapists and the world around you can make you feel like it is all in your head, a problem with you. But being around people who felt the same, who attributed it to the same causes, you thought maybe the problem was the world, not you – it made you feel less alone. Part of something bigger.

4

Healing

The new world we build must not only create powerful collective bodies, but must ensure that its parts – us – are autonomous, empowered and cared for also. To do so, we look here more closely at the specifics of the human mind and body.

A perspective on the mind often associated with complexity theory, which has already been heavily implied in the previous chapters, is that developed by Chilean biologists Humberto Maturana and Francisco Varela, known as the Santiago theory of cognition. In this perspective, mind is not seen as a thing but as a process. As we have seen, bodies receive input from their environment, activate structures, and adapt, something that occurs in everything from a single-celled organism to a human, to a city. This sensing is an aspect of cognition. Over time, the body evolves in coupling with this environment. It adapts to access those elements most relevant to its survival, such as how bats and dogs have higher frequency hearing than humans. And at the same time the body shapes the environment through its interactions, as in how we have designed technology and culture around our hearing range. In this double sense, cognition involves a body creating its own 'world', both internally and externally. This cognition is sometimes referred to as being 4E: embodied, embedded, extended and enactive. Given the much broader definition of 'body' we have used that already extends beyond the human, we can cover all of these with *the embodied mind*.

As a side note, a beautiful irony presents itself here. Like the Santiago theory of cognition, the right-wing shock doctrine not only grew out of experiments on the human mind, but was also first applied in Santiago, Chile, following the US-supported coup by General Pinochet. It seems appropriate that the inversion of the shock doctrine presented in this book should emerge from the very place that it started.

Unhealthy Relations

It was late at the UCL campus, and the meeting was tense. We found ourselves a quiet room in a dark, labyrinthine old building, empty apart from us and the occasional cleaner. On entering, the group had spontaneously polarized, moving towards opposite ends of the table. The dispute we had come together to try to resolve had been growing for months, and it was harming our daily organizing and mental health. Yet, despite how unlikely it had felt at the beginning of the meeting, by its end we had made good progress. What had become a mutually hurtful situation of escalating intensity, much of it conducted online, was rapidly diffused with that oldest and most obvious technology: talking and listening face-to-face.

The connection we feel to animated, human faces responding to our words proves vital in organizing. The face aids in providing care, in healing from hurt, for apologizing and making amends, for enthusing and empowering others. It provides immediate feedback on our actions, enabling our bodies to adapt together in the moment. Communications technology has many advantages, but the loss of the human face – animated and responsive rather than a frozen avatar – is a threat to resilient organizing.

For one thing it amplifies an existing tendency of conflict. In these situations we often see the other side in simplified terms, an enemy, without considering the parts, the past experiences, the imagined futures, the environments and interactions, empowerments and disempowerments which brought each side to that point. This obscures the reasons why conflict occurred, and makes it difficult to adapt to ensure that it is not repeated. To be transformative, conflict resolution has to proceed, as difficult as it may be, through an understanding of all the bodies involved.

Internal conflict can also act as an accelerator of positive growth, rather than just of collapse. By creating space in which people can express their position without judgement, you can help to uncover aspects of a body that are harmful or oppressive. You allow individuals to see the effects they may not have realized they were creating, and allow them to change. And we will often come to the realization that the triggering event has beneath it much longer histories of trauma and oppression.

Scars on the Body

'Sorry that I keep talking about the eviction', my friend said, hunched over his pint. 'I just haven't been able to think about much else recently.'

Housing campaigners had gone through a tumultuous year. Despite previously resisting eviction, the occupation of a housing block in north London earmarked for demolition ended in one final, violent showdown with the bailiffs. Months had now passed. Whenever I bumped into people from the occupation, they all seemed fixed on that moment: the trauma of the violence, of losing a place you had built your life around, the end of the future paths you had imagined. Yet also how empowering it had been.

'They tried to bury us; they didn't know we were seeds', announced the Latin-American proverb that adorned their largest banner. 'And now the seeds have scattered', my friend said hopefully. One just hopes these seeds were not too damaged by the experience to grow. A few involved had dropped out of political activity for a while afterwards. Which is, of course, one of the goals of police repression, of spurious arrests, intimidation and violent coercion: to shock your body, to send it into chaos, to disempower you.

Trauma is embodied. It is re-lived in its triggers and flashbacks, in the whole body replaying the past in the present. Heart rate, oxygen intake, dilated pupils, spike of stress hormones. Amplified responses to stimuli. Dissociation, the feeling of not being there. Yet there is nothing 'irrational' about this; so far as the past experience of the body is concerned, it is acting in order to survive. Either way, the body's ability to relate productively to others or itself is compromised – it is socially disempowered.

Trauma is embodied not just in the individual, but in collective bodies too. Not long after the tragic fire at Grenfell Tower, I was passing nearby and decided to walk over to see if I could find a friend of mine, a Radical Housing Network activist who had lived there and miraculously escaped the blaze. As the charred outline of the tower finally looms into view, it hits you in the gut. The streets were full of people, shifting supplies to and from churches, holding vigils, singing, placing flowers, pinning up missing persons' posters, children's drawings, Bible verses. I could not find my friend and left fairly quickly, worried that I was intruding on collective grief.

When people are torn away from us like this, the emotional loss we feel is joined by a wider loss, of the part they played in empowering the community. A teacher, a doctor, a shopkeeper, a gardener, a friend or a family member, each leaving a hole in their community. The landscape, too, functions as part of the extended mind, constantly reminding of the past. Yet collective traumas also become focal points, which a community can come together around and create new healing relationships, such as the 'disaster communism' of self-organized aid that follows in the aftermath of events like Hurricane Sandy.

We can even see traumas on the global level, in the long-term feuds of international relations that erupt in war and genocide; or in the 'metabolic rift' that capitalist environmental abuse creates in the earth's natural cycles. And like individual traumas, whether we will be able to find healing after these global traumas will depend on our capacity to form empowered global bodies able to act.

Power to Act, and Power Over Others

If wholes emerge from ordering parts, and a coherent path of change emerges from an ordered vision, consider the tension this creates: enabling one thing always requires constraining another. To order a part, you constrain the vast array of other places it could be. To fix a path, you cut off all the other possible futures you could head towards.

The human emerges out of the interaction of its parts, but that whole human decides where those body parts will travel. The layout of the city which has emerged from the residents' interactions will influence where later residents will live, work and play. The shared culture that emerges in a social group constrains what is considered acceptable behaviour. You might question today how we lived before smartphones, because this technology that emerged and spread has been reshaping the world around it to make it essential to everyday life. We can see here two directions of power:

Power-to is the ability of a body to interact with others in order to create larger wholes.

Power-over is the ability of larger social bodies to constrain their parts.

We often describe one human as having power over another. I would argue that this is best understood as a shorthand, as this is only possible by virtue of being able to activate the power-over of a larger social body. A father in a traditional family is able to exercise power over other family members not merely because of his physical strength, but from his greater power to leverage the wider bodies that order the family, through controlling flows of money, or laws and social attitudes that favour men. A landlord has power over a tenant only because of his power to engage a larger body – the state – to remove someone for not paying rent. Likewise, a person of colour can rightfully feel that a white person has power over them, because of similar disparities of power in relation to the state, the media, or general public opinion.

Our vision of the future likewise has power over us. If we believe there is 'no alternative' to neoliberalism, we lose all reason to fight. If we fear the consequences of an action, we are less likely to do it. When we are already on a particular path – our career, family, friendships – then options are judged against those existing futures. If it does not offer clear relation to our hopes and desires, an option will seem less relevant to our lives, and we are less likely to engage. The futures we see in the present set us on a path to creating them, but can also obscure alternative possibilities.

Engines of Oppression

We are born into already constituted systems of norms, for example around gender, which exercise power over us. While these do not fully determine us, they do shape our development in everything from clothing, hairstyle, vocal style, beliefs about intelligence and worth, rights and sexual expression. Pushing against this can be hard work.

Deviations from those norms can seem strange, even threatening; the queer person causes a kind of chaos in that heterosexual symbolic order, a destruction of meaning. This sense of threat, disgust or confusion is often responded to through mockery, intimidation or physical violence. That of course imprints on the recipient's body as trauma, making it less likely that they will openly express themselves in future.

Gender norms therefore act as a kind of balancing mechanism, where deviations are identified and crushed. Cycles that minimize differences, slowing down production of change, we might call *decelerators* (a.k.a 'negative feedback loops'). This is in contrast to accelerators ('positive feedback loops'), which speed up growth or collapse by amplifying change.

The complex whole of an oppressive system is criss-crossed by cycles which both speed up collapse and crush difference. This can be seen in the production of 'surplus' populations. In a capitalist system, feeding our metabolisms to survive requires money, given as payment for doing a job. We are beholden therefore to the standards imposed by employers. Those who are less well-versed in standard middle-class rules of behaviour, who struggled at school, who are mentally ill, or who are physically unable to work a standard eight-hour day – these people are far less likely to find stable income. Without the means to support themselves, these people are expelled from the social body. They are effectively part of the entropy of capitalism, those who could not be ordered to the system's liking, so must be flushed out.

The police then act as the white blood cells of the capitalist body. Activated at any sign of disorder, and using 'lawful' repression – such as protecting private property or 'public decency' – they cleanse the social body of this entropic population. Prison – as well as death from violent policing – produces a cycle of further community trauma, breaking up families and friends and local ties of support, putting further lives into chaos, pushing people closer towards homelessness, drug addiction and imprisonment. Once marginalized, people can become quickly entangled in loops that flatten difference from social norms and accelerate collapse in their ability to survive.

A system of oppression is therefore an active, present process, even where it relies on traumatic histories. Both must be dealt with. If we reform processes that reproduce, for example, racial segregation – the justice system, the media, capitalist exploitation – the psychological imprint of power on our bodies remains, and so may unconsciously reappear in other ways. Conversely, even if the bodily imprint of oppression is removed, the underlying active capitalist processes will remain, and will produce those oppressions again over time.

Fighting Power is Work

I rested for a moment on the cold concrete floor of the warehouse, struggling to hear our discussion over the din of the others. Facilitating a participatory discussion can be hard work, particularly with over a hundred people but, as exhausted as I was, the event was going well. The topic was utopias, and we had broken into groups to talk on a different subtopic each: housing, environment, media, education and so on. Despite the subject matter, however, the power dynamics shown in how people were interacting in these groups were not all so utopian.

Equitable patterns do not always form spontaneously in social situations. The more confident people will often be louder, and often those will be men, they will be white, they will be middle class. We bring in to social spaces the powers inscribed on our bodies from elsewhere, and it takes vigilance to minimize. In formal settings, a facilitator or meeting chair can assist, bringing in extra order, clarifying shared rules, encouraging those less confident. A temporary group body has its own path that can be steered, away from dominating behaviour and towards a distributed empowerment. But this requires *work*.

We commonly understand work in the sense of 'doing a job for pay'. But work is also the word used in thermodynamics for transfers of energy. The water that spins a waterwheel is performing work. The swing of a hammer by human hand is work. As is my brain converting glucose into neuron activity to process thoughts as I construct this sentence. This is a purely mechanical sense of work, however; it is inadequate for explaining more abstract social power. Trying to deal with an argumentative partner when out shopping might feel like harder 'work' than doing it alone, even if both use the same amount of physical energy.

In attempting to bridge this gap, neuroscientist Terrence Deacon gives a more general definition of work, which captures both the physical and the social. Work for Deacon is 'the production of contragrade change'. By contragrade he means change which is *opposite to the tendency of that body*. The extent to which a body creates changes that would not occur spontaneously is the amount of work that has taken place. An office worker changing databases, making phone calls, and trying to solve problems is performing work, as they are producing change which would not occur spontaneously, even if largely digital, communicative and mental rather than physical. This definition also covers activities that are often unjustly ignored as work, such as care for children, elderly and disabled people – all of which are work, regardless of being paid or not.

Caution is needed, however. Work is now expanded to the extent that it can include starting a fight with a stranger, or indeed just sitting and imagining the details of such a fight. The feeling of struggling against oppression is affirmed as work, but then so is going out of your way to actively harm others. Power-to and power-over between any bodies involves work, meaning that work can be produced without awareness, like a community as a whole producing an oppressive environment without anyone consciously trying to.

It might seem that this breadth makes the term useless, but that is in fact its very use: it destroys the possibility of attaching value to work in and of itself. In her book *The Problem with Work*, Kathi Weeks argues that if we aim to create a future free from the drudgery of wage labour, we cannot simply argue that, for example, 'care work is work' or 'sex work is work' and imply they should be valued for that reason alone, because that still entails that *work is inherently valuable*. Our alternative definition of work in contrast shows that work is *not* inherently valuable, and provides a material explanation for this.

To judge whether work is valuable we need to consider not only whether the path of a body has changed, but also where those different paths would take us. Given our present state of multi-scalar disorder and collapse, threatening the very basis of human life – and thus of any ethical judgement – I would argue that work can be seen as valuable to the extent that it is directed against that collapse. In other words, does it contribute to a movement towards a more resilient and empowered world at multiple scales? Considering multiple scales is important to warn us against, for example, fighting against global ecological disaster by enabling fascist or colonial policies, or fighting against a government's economic policy while encouraging or ignoring local violence against LGBT people.

Work is 'bullshit' to the extent that it works against this resilience or health. Digging a hole and filling it in may be equivalent work in energy terms to helping bathe an elderly patient, but the former is not essential to the creation of resilient bodies like the latter is. We need food; we do not need advertising or management consultancy. And we cannot just say that reproducing a body is valuable work, if that body (such as a corporation) is then destroying others through its practices. We have to examine the relations between bodies and the cumulative effects of our actions. The value of work is then no longer determined by the capitalist metric of profit, nor is it merely defined in opposition to that metric. Work is valued for its ability to create a path towards a resilient world.

We can even retain a sort of work ethic, a sense of 'we must all contribute to society', a fairness of effort – but one which takes into account our separate abilities. In current disability-rights discourse, people talk about the 'spoons' they have remaining, an informal measure of the energy one has to fulfil day-to-day tasks like doing the washing up or leaving the house. *Spoons are lost through work* – even if that work is mental rather than physical, and even if the same task by a non-disabled person could be performed with little work. Effort that one person expends helping another to regain their 'spoons' is therefore more valuable than the same time spent supporting someone who does not need it. And it is certainly more valuable than any work done to deprive people of their survival.

Finally, ethical judgements about work must take

into account a distinction which has been implicit in this chapter, between cognition and *consciousness*. A nation state may be a cognitive body, in its sensing and adapting to events – but it does not *feel*, like we do. It does not reach out to us and say 'that protest really hurt my feelings'. Consciousness is a particularly intense form of cognition, where a sensing body becomes aware of itself sensing, and aware even of itself sensing that sensing. This reflexive complexity enables the feeling of (and reflection on) pain, fear, joy and hope, beyond mere unconscious reaction to stimuli. It makes conscious bodies the ethical focus of our work.

The explorations in this chapter answer the earlier objection to the body model, that its language risked reflecting the neoliberal shock doctrine. Body metaphors that ignore the difference between conscious parts (e.g. humans) and non-conscious parts (e.g. heart, lungs etc), imply that equivalent 'surgical' interventions are justified in social bodies as in patients in the emergency room. Our model avoids this problem, by locating ethical focus not only in the social whole, but spread across its conscious parts, in all their feelings of trauma and disempowerment.

By foregrounding both the autonomy of cognition and the felt experience of consciousness, the

Shock Doctrine of the Left wards off tyrannical uses of the strategy. With this in mind, we now turn to examine how we engage with the most potentially tyrannical body of them all: the state.

Further Reading

The Body Keeps the Score: Brain, Mind, and Body in the Healing of Trauma by Bessel van der Kolk is a scientifically rigorous yet readable and open-minded work exploring the embodied effects of trauma. *Incomplete Nature: How Mind Emerged from Matter* by Terrence Deacon presents a detailed model bridging the physical, mental and social worlds, exploring how a body's path is pulled towards its future ('teleodynamics'), and providing support for our definitions of work and consciousness. *INCITE community accountability resources* (available at http://www.incite-national.org) provide useful tools for creating community justice systems beyond the state. *Social Reproduction Theory: Remapping Class, Recentering Oppression*, edited by Tithi Bhattacharya, highlights the many cycles of work – often unpaid and under-appreciated – which recreate social bodies.

Interlude

Polling day. It is late, but the library is quiet. Following the arrows to a side room, you approach the clerks' table, and they hand you a slip of paper. You walk over to one of the booths, and place a tick next to the most progressive candidate. You did not recognize the name, but you were not about to vote for any other party.

A strange process. All the participatory democratic processes you had become used to in the past few years made it frustratingly clear how antiquated and unempowering this system was. No use in protesting it tonight though. You posted the slip into the ballot box and headed home to get ready for the party.

You were on the bus when the exit polls were released – the Tories with the most seats as expected, but with huge losses that were not. Social media went berserk and you nearly missed your stop from staring at your phone. The party was still buzzing with shock when you arrived. Another group of friends came shortly after, fresh from knocking on doors to get the vote out. Before Corbyn many in your circles scoffed at the idea that electoral politics was empowering, but it was hard to deny when it had led so many people into their first ever political activity. You could see it in their bodies. It wasn't enough, but it was something – it kicked up energy, even in the anarchists who opposed it. The question remained, however, as to whether this energy could be channelled into broader revolutionary movement, or if electoral projects were always doomed to eventual disappointment . . .

5

Taming

The previous chapters have focused on action from outside the state: attacking enemy bodies, creating new alternatives, repairing the relations in our existing communities. Action *within* the state – such as through elections – is a more contentious topic, as it represents a point at which parts of the left sharply diverge. Either way, given the wide-ranging impact of electoral politics, as well as the state's ability to hinder our other interventions, we stand to benefit from investigating its dynamics more closely.

Approaches to the state are often categorized as either reformist or revolutionary: you either aim to use the existing state to gradually tame the excesses of capitalism, or you wish to suddenly smash it whole and create something new in its place. Problems with the latter should be clear from the previous chapters – the huge unpredictability caused by chaos, the need to have alternatives already built, and the potential cycles of trauma caused by wide-scale violence.

But there are very good reasons to dismiss reformism as well. Change brought through parliamentary politics tends to be slow, incremental, and easily reversible. Reforms often patch up surface problems without dealing with their root causes. And being at the whim of the electoral cycle, while creating rapid mobilization at first, also brings unavoidable demobilization, rarely translating into a sustainable, organized movement beyond election day.

The dichotomy is unhelpful, and forces us to choose between one of two bad options. Looking more closely at the dynamics of the state body can help us develop a strategy that avoids the pitfalls of both.

The State's Senses

On one occasion, I was certain that an eager new recruit was a police spy. I had little or no proof beyond my own paranoia, but something about them just did not sit right. Out of place in almost every way, in how they dressed, talked, how they filled the space of the room. Overly enthusiastic despite no experience, seemingly little knowledge of left politics. A very bare and recently created social-media profile.

But wasn't that what we wanted, to mobilize new people, more than the usual suspects? New faces should be welcomed, but instead here I was withdrawing from an enthusiastic new activist. A paranoid, self-isolating reflex: 'They are trying to be helpful. What's wrong with them?'

Then occasionally something happens to remind you that yes, we are spied on. Friends have their faces splashed across a tabloid after being secretly filmed. A recently exposed spy cop turns out to have been a member of an organization you had just joined. Police officers address an older comrade by name at a protest before they have even spoken, and you see footage of a masked 'protester' walking unmolested behind police lines. Paranoia does not help, but neither does naivety.

The state sees you. From statistics collected on labour, crime, housing, education, immigration; from polling and reaction to current events received via the media and foreign governments; to ubiquitous electronic and CCTV surveillance. Its arms reach into the world and feed information back to the centre on what is happening. It has learned responses to these changes from its past activity. And it intervenes to bring things back onto the path it sees for the future, through laws, regulations, fiscal and monetary policy, police mobilization and war. The state is a body.

When you sense, you do not take in everything from your environment, just what your body has evolved to see as relevant. All bodies reduce complexity in this way, and the state is no exception. State projects of standardization have shaped everything from personal names and city layouts, to measurements, languages and forests; anything in a body and their surroundings that is available is categorized and measured.

When the state intervenes back into the world, it does so on the basis of these simplified models, recreating the very rigid order that it at first imagined existed. Given its size and deep integration into so many aspects of society, including its monopoly on violence, the state now enjoys an unparalleled power to re-order the bodies that fall within and around it. It moulds not only material infrastructure but also common sense, through state broadcasters, the close coupling of business elites to government, through setting curriculums, funding for universities and research and so on. Little is left untouched by this grid of simplification and rigidity, including our sense of self.

The state is therefore ill-equipped to respond to complexity or diversity in its parts. Policy applies here and everywhere, local differences be damned. Whether it is the absurdly simplistic solution of Brexit leading to economic meltdown, or the disastrous forced collectivization of agriculture under Stalin, both failures can in part be seen as blowback from states' attempts to reduce the complexity of their environments.

The alternative to simplifying an environment is to increase your own internal complexity – including the ability to sense – to match it. Say you are at work, and you are given too many tasks to do at once, leading to you getting overwhelmed and failing to complete any of them. Increasing the number of workers would help to prevent this collapse. Too many cooks may spoil the broth, but too few cooks and the broth may not even get made. This balance is the 'law of requisite variety', or the First Law of Cybernetics

Witness how states have responded to the multiple crises of the twenty-first century, particularly around immigration and terrorism: increasing rigidity of borders (simplification of the flows of people from outside), while expanding the 'surveillance state' both online and offline (increased complexity of sensing). This occurs also in socialist states. To defend from threats – both actual and imagined – from people who oppose a revolution, states have often closed borders and repressed trade unions and newspapers (reducing external unpredictability), while also expanding state bureaucracy and surveillance (increasing internal complexity).

An alternative means of expanding internal complexity would be decentralization of power, allowing multiple autonomous centres of sensing and adaptation guided by local knowledge. The centralized state is fundamentally incapable of surmounting our current complex crises, and must be replaced with a more participatory, decentralized and adaptable structure in order for us to survive.

If it ultimately needs to be replaced, however, a question remains: is it possible to use the state to bring about its own end?

Imagine you are walking a familiar route through a forest. The walk is easy, the ground having been beaten down by the stomp of a thousand feet, a path cleared away through the trees. How much harder to advance it would be to leave the path, and to claw your way through the tangled bushes. Leaving a path becomes difficult once it has set in. Your regular route becomes progressively more ordered, easier to navigate with fewer obstacles. From the difficulty of changing your daily habits, to creating a temporary name for your band and it accidentally sticking, to how QWERTY remains the standard layout for keyboards. Once you have set out on a path, it creates its own pull: path dependence, or lock-in.

Lock-in presents a problem for those parts of the left that plan for a spontaneous 'withering away' of the state. Given the path of increasing global complexity, the need for expanding internal state complexity in response will always push the state in the opposite direction to withering away, whether controlled by the left or the right. If the state is to be used for revolutionary purposes, there has to be a clearer plan for how this path can be broken.

No Turning Back

Night falls while you are walking in the forest, and you are lost. The darkness is so thick you cannot see the ground beneath you. You stand frozen, unsure of where any movement will lead. If you take a step forward, how far will you move? If it is flat ground, you will move slightly forward. If you are on a curb, you will feel a sudden but small change in height. A steep incline, and you will feel the force of gravity make you rush to the bottom. Or perhaps you are on a cliff edge, and your step forward will send you plummeting to the bottom. The only way to find out is to try.

For each change, returning the same way presents different challenges. A small step downwards and you could move back with little effort. The sharper incline you could walk slowly back up, but it would take much more effort. But falling off a cliff, presuming you survived, would prevent you from returning the same way. Only the latter change is irreversible – not that you cannot get back to the same place, but that you must take a different route to get there.

Your body contains many similar thresholds: when you fall asleep, when you are too full of food to keep eating, when you pass your alcohol limit and suddenly find yourself uncontrollably drunk. You may only creep over the threshold, and yet the change of body state can be dramatic. The most dramatic threshold of course, is death. Likewise, reforms can have varying steepness of change. A carbon tax might be like the curb, not changing much and easily reversible; whereas a debt jubilee could significantly affect the economy and is impossible to immediately reverse – it would take time to re-accumulate the level of debt that was written off.

Being easily reversible does not make a reform

bad – anti-discrimination law for example – but it does mean we take great risks in focusing solely on them. To utilize reforms while avoiding *reformism*, we have to give greater weight to those which create or open up the possibility of irreversible change. But the extent of irreversibility involves more than just the reform itself, and even relatively reversible reforms can be strengthened by shaping common sense around them.

Bodies of Knowledge

Jeremy Corbyn came to my hometown. I remained cautious about electoral projects, but political events did not usually happen there, and my parents had become fans, so I made it an excuse to visit. I do not recall much from the rally, other than that it was hard to disagree with much that Corbyn said. I remember my mother offering me a sweet from her pocket. I remember holding on to my father's arm to steady him. And I remember the feeling of pride, as I glanced over at my parents at every moment of applause, to see them nodding along.

Later at home, we sat in their cosy living room chatting over glasses of red wine, getting progressively drunk and animated. They talked about their childhoods, the poverty they had experienced. About the royal family, though they had never liked them, apart from Diana. How all people should be treated with the respect they gave to you, except for the taxman, the courts and the council, who were all money-grubbing jobsworths. The British Empire did some nasty things didn't it? And once they were drunk enough to feel no shame in talking party politics, they mentioned how – until this year – they had always voted Conservative.

My mother began the night balking at the word 'communism'. As more wine was drunk, she told me she could never be a communist; she'd grown up under it and knew what it was like. More wine was drunk, and more, until she was joyously bellowing Yugoslav patriotic songs they learned as children, and saying how much they used to love Tito. It was all about the beauty of nature and the people wasn't it, she said, and isn't that better than God Save the Queen? My dad agreed. He didn't like what they ended up doing in Russia, but maybe it wouldn't always be like that. They say Jesus was sort of a communist don't they? I swigged back my glass, hiding the satisfied smirk on my face.

Can someone be a shy Tory and a shy communist simultaneously? Perhaps political positions are not quite as clearcut as they are often made out to be. Although the existence of parties and political culture will shape us from above, our individual politics are ultimately unique, the result of parts – experiences, desires, demands – which interact to produce a whole. We can see the meaning that emerges out of human and collective bodies as itself a sort of body; not physical, but conceptual.

Cognitive psychologists talk of these bodies of knowledge in terms of 'schemas', where our minds pull together conceptual parts into a whole. Our cognitive schema of the concept 'holiday' is not just a written definition, but involves the triggering of related concepts. Mine involves a beach, a parasol, deck chairs, flying kites, ice cream. Someone else's might involve a jungle or a cruise ship, or a previous traumatic experience. My current model for 'communism' includes large meetings full of ordinary people, collective farming, robots, leisure time. For those on the right it may be emaciated gulag prisoners, bread lines, assassinations. Each is built out of our experiences around the concept, and so varies in details. Associations can change, however, so struggle around meanings is always ongoing.

It is not only that whole concepts like 'communism' can be differently interpreted, but also how their parts can be combined in wildly different ways. Two people may share a concern for their children's health or preserving the countryside, yet arrive at very different political support on the strength of that concern, as alliances between environmental activists and rural Conservatives demonstrate. If we can identify where parts are shared between otherwise contradictory bodies, we have a means to create common ground.

This common ground is not simply to 'bridge differences', but to change them. By finding ways of interacting with those otherwise opposed to us, we have greater influence in their evolution. Attacking an individual's whole body of knowledge at once ensures they will stop listening. But using those inroads to create an empathetic link, seeding parts of your own perspective, and then undermining their original position, is more effective. You might say *Building* an alternative framework in their mind based on *Healing* existing concerns before *Smashing* the one that previously dominated.

Couples

Although persuasion is important in building movement, we must recognize when the effort is not worth it. Thus the contemporary question: should we debate with Nazis?

There is a difference between active fascist organizers, passive supporters of racist government policy, and neutral parties who have not really formed an opinion. Trying to persuade the latter groups is necessary; the former is a waste of time. Fascist organizers are closely coupled to a central body that is reproducing those ideas. The closer they are, the more their psychological organization is *ordered* by that other body.

Take a romantic couple. You begin as two very different people, albeit with enough similarities to attract you to one another. Over time, you continue to adapt to your environments, only now you experience them more frequently in the same way: going to places together, reacting to events, meeting friends and family. That person becomes a regular feature of your life, someone you expect to be there. Your social, psychological and even physical metabolisms become entwined. They become, if you will, part of your extended body. Their absence can be felt as an absence within you, and an injury to them can likewise feel like your own.

So coupling is always double edged: necessary for creating a shared path, but at the risk of becoming dependent on one another, and being vulnerable to their vulnerabilities. Extending this to a political body on the left, take the UK activist group Momentum. On the one hand, its close coupling to the Labour Party, and particularly Corbyn, has allowed it to influence its evolution, pulling it to the left and massively popularizing socialist ideas. At the same time, this coupling is a weakness. Actions will always be based around Labour, and any shock that hits one can reverberate through the other. At the time of writing it is unclear what might happen to Momentum should Corbyn step down; it will be interesting to see whether it has developed enough autonomy and a clear path to survive.

Releasing Pressure

When a dynamic body begins a new path, initially surrounded by many potentials, it tends towards streamlining and simplifying its order. You move into a new area, and the bewildering array of places and people eventually narrows down to regular friends, your favourite shops, your daily route to the train station and so on. In an economy, companies develop supply chains, internal processes and culture, their niches narrow as they adapt to competition in the market. Scientific disciplines over time create narrower and narrower specializations. All involve the gradual forming of order out of previous chaos.

But these paths contain the seeds of their own collapse. As efficiency rises, resilience falls. You accumulate, slowing what were fluid relations in ordered stocks: knowledge assumed as correct, relationships which become routine, or the accumulation of capital in a narrowing group of people. This gradually leads to rigidity and loss of adaptability, whether across an economy or in your own mind. Unexpected shocks become more likely to cause fatal collapse. When collapse occurs, all those connections are flung apart, sending the cycle into a creative chaotic stage, before it eventually returns to expanding along a more defined path.

This pattern of rapid growth, conservation, release and reorganization is known as the adaptive cycle. It is seen in everything from the 'creative destruction' of the business cycle, to the sweeping of fires through densely packed forests, to the 'paradigm shifts' observed in scientific knowledge.

This tendency can, however, be diverted, and often is. Instead of waiting for a huge collapse in the whole, deliberate smaller collapses can be created to break apart rigid links and introduce flexibility. This is why forest managers will deliberately start small fires to reduce density, in order to prevent larger uncontrollable fires in the future.

Elections are one such means of doing this in a social system. When a government is young, the future feels open, with many opportunities and possibilities; years down the line, however, they will have accumulated many associations of failure, broken promises, scandals and so on. As time goes on, people will increasingly lose faith in that government. However, once every few years, all those connections are broken apart. New faces are elected, weak links are cast off, popular ones remain, cabinets are reshuffled, and the nation is reinvigorated with a sense of potential.

This is one reason for the relative resilience and perceived legitimacy of liberal democracy: conserved energy is released in controlled, deliberate collapses, rather than a sudden total release, such as at the end of a decades-long dictatorship. One might argue that this therefore gives better account-ability to public concerns, but it is difficult not to lament how it ultimately strengthens an otherwise broken system, derailing potentially revolutionary energy in order to 'give the other lot a chance'.

Either way, those deliberate collapses cause chaos, and so open up the possibility of directing change, whichever party is in power. Being prepared for the effects of elections is therefore necessary, even for those who would otherwise wish to abstain from party politics. The alternative is simply to be swept up by its waves without any control whatsoever.

The Shock Doctrine of the Left must reject incremental reformism which keeps us locked into the current path of the state. Neither, however, should it rely on totalizing shock to break away from such a path – 'smashing the state' – which leaves us vulnerable to hugely unpredictable chaos. This dilemma can be overcome through coordinating smaller but escalating shocks, each time increasing the power of people to organize beyond the state.

The rapid and irreversible reforms of neoliberal shock must be matched by left governments. Those reforms cannot of course involve privatization and decreased public spending, but neither can they simply repeat the centralizing state socialist reforms of the past. The state must however be understood not as a neutral tool to be taken, but as an autonomous body with its own trajectory that cannot be fully controlled, one that can sweep up even the most principled of left-wing politicians. The 'taming' therefore should be seen not only as what the state can do to capitalism, but what the grassroots movement must also do to the state.

Taming

This concludes the last of our four lenses. These previous chapters have examined the dynamics of direct action, organization building, emotion and social democracy. The task of our final chapter is to combine these into a coherent meta-strategy.

Further Reading

Seeing Like a State by James C. Scott demonstrates the rigid order in state sensing, and its creation of environments that match that rigidity. *Designing Freedom* by Stafford Beer introduces cybernetic concepts such as the law of requisite variety. Beer also provides a link into shock doctrine history, as the architect of socialist Chile's utopian visions prior to the coup. *Resilience Thinking* and *Resilience Practice* by Brian Walker and David Salt explains the adaptive cycle and the notion of thresholds. *Hegemony How-To: A Roadmap for Radicals* by Jonathan Smucker is a great resource for outward-focused, persuasive organizing.

6

The Meta-Strategy

Different strategies of the left tend to privilege some of the four logics over the others. Where these are not coordinated, tensions can arise. *Smashing* actions can unintentionally harm bodies we wish to preserve, whether through creating power vacuums, trauma, or retaliation. *Building* of a social movement body may reproduce internal power relations that others are struggling against, such as how leftist organizations can nonetheless be racist, sexist, ableist and so on. Communities focused on *Healing* may develop processes to protect people from oppressed and traumatized backgrounds that are ethically laudable, but become increasingly impenetrable to outsiders, and so hamper growth. And *Taming* dominant powers through the state comes at the risk of empowering the very bodies which seek to repress and demobilize the movement.

Only by coordinating these different parts can we overcome these tensions, and so create an emergent whole strategy.

Before we continue to proposals for movement organization and its speculative future path, a word of caution. If the book has been taken seriously up to now, then it will be clear that these suggestions *must not be taken as a static blueprint*. It is a possible future of the social movement as seen from the vantage point of the present, and from my geographical position. As new presents emerge, our visions and strategies must be reviewed, and adapted, based on the success or failure of its parts. While there are certain mechanisms we can identify and apply across time and space, there can never be a blueprint for revolution.

This final chapter is merely an application to the present of the toolset presented in the previous chapters. In terms of being a successful strategy, it may be wrong; in fact it almost certainly is. The task is to begin testing these ideas, and adapting them until they do work. I merely offer a suggestion for where we may begin. So, without further ado:

The Meta-Strategy

From Parts to Whole

The logics can work together even as they remain differentiated, if each forms its own accelerating loop feeding into the same internal movement.

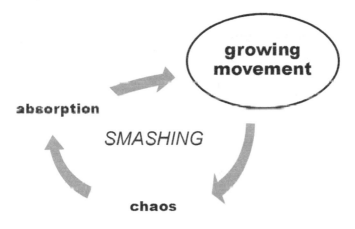

In moments of chaos, new people become mobilized. Preparing a regular and reliable system of absorption – through training and DNA – allows us to guide these people quickly to where they are most needed. The movement grows, and larger actions become possible, setting up an accelerating cycle. This is the core catalyst of movement growth, which all the other cycles rely on.

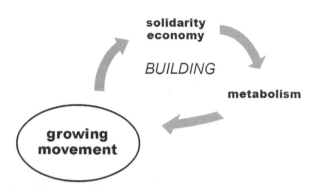

Extra capacity is also siphoned into building alternative institutions, with workers' cooperatives, housing cooperatives and social centres supporting each other to create a sustainable solidarity economy. These in turn support the metabolism of the wider movement: providing spaces to organize, food and resources to maintain occupations and strikes and so on. As the capacity for action grows, so does the capacity to support it materially.

Others can be directed towards organizing support groups, caucuses, social events, and training in mediation, accountability, power and privilege. This makes for a more resilient movement, minimizing the entropy of burnout, marginalization and conflict, and so again strengthens and stabilizes the movement.

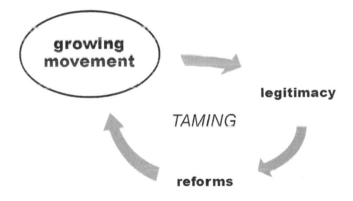

And, as the movement grows, by engaging with mainstream media and political institutions (even as an antagonistic outsider) it gains legitimacy as a political force, and finds wider reach. It is then more likely to see the reforms it wants, specifically those which increase the strength and autonomy of the movement.

Each logic is therefore contributing to a growing

movement, without interfering with the autonomy of groups or individuals.

While this would certainly bring greater consistency to the movement, I believe another step is needed to create a cohesive body that acts together on a shared path. As we have seen, lots of isolated parts all linking into one central body is an unresilient structure. Little interaction between the parts leads to inadequate building of social and emotional connections. And conflicts between the logics are inevitable, particularly around the contentious role of the state versus those taking direct action. Without further cohesive structure this arrangement risks falling apart.

I therefore propose four principles which cross over the different logics, a common ground to provide cohesion to the strategy. These are derived from the discussions in the previous chapters: the organizational form of the *ecology of organizations*; the utilization of chaos for directing that whole body which I call *accelerating action*; an underlying *care ethic*; and an orientation towards the state that favours *autonomy-supporting reforms*.

Ecology of Organizations

All parts of the left should seek to develop and participate in an ecology of organizations. By this I mean a network of autonomous organizations that share no single organizational form, but which come together in a sustained pattern. It favours neither the hierarchical revolutionary party, nor the localized action group. Instead, the organizational form of any part will be shaped by both its local needs and its function within the ecology, rather than a dogmatic assertion of some ideal form. The focus is on how to work better together, how to become more resilient and collectively effective over a longer period of time. There should be no place in the ecology for self-serving, competitive, parasitic or uncharitable behaviour. How an action will build and support the rest of the ecology is as important a consideration as the effect it will have on yourselves.

The ecology must both resist and aim to replace current power. Not a coalition of campaign groups alone, nor just trade unions, cooperatives, or NGOs, but networks which bring these together and create active relations between them. Not merely an abstract agreement, a name added to a list of supporters on a website, but the development of functional social economies which share skills, resources and platforms. The radical hairdressing salon should be able to play as important a part in this as the alternative media centre or the anti-fascist action group.

I borrow the term 'ecology' to contribute to an ongoing discussion around this term, though it may be more accurate and in keeping with our model to call this a 'body of bodies'. For one, I emphasize an element of this body-of-social-movement-bodies that is not normally associated with ecology: its formalization through DNA. Shared formal coding could create a more cohesive and powerful whole, allowing rapid and sustainable growth, while maintaining both the autonomy of groups and a shared direction.

The Story would be a broad and highly accessible description of our current world and a vivid picture of a better future. This is best developed collectively, although in line with the previous chapters I would argue for an initial focus on things like collective ownership and control of workplaces, empowering participatory democracy and so on.

The long-term Strategy I would argue for would naturally be that set out in this concluding chapter, although again simplified and made as accessible as possible without destroying its core elements.

The Structure requires more specific suggestions.

As well as the fluid networking properties, the ecology also needs formal, geographically situated democratic structures beneath. As much as the internet has broadened our communicative reach, we must remember that workplaces are still generally physical *places,* as are communities, as are the human bodies needed for causing disruption. Digital tools for making democratic engagement more accessible should of course be utilized, but the structures must be based around locality.

The growth of the ecology would not, however, be controlled by these democratic organs. The DNA would allow these structures to spread in a self-organized, decentralized manner, while maintaining enough coherence in their structure and ideology to link into this wider federation.

The internal democracy could take many forms,

but I would nonetheless suggest that alongside a nesting of assemblies, there be a sortition-based guiding coalition.

'Guiding coalition' implies not a hierarchical leadership as in a central committee, but a body whose job it is to ensure the health of the ecology – its mandated 'body builder'. Members from the guiding module tour the ecology, creating personal relationships, finding problems, facilitating dialogue between groups, collecting the information that allows the assemblies to make decisions on strategy.

'Sortition' involves random selection, as in jury duty, from a pool of people willing to take on important roles. This is mixed with a number of directly elected delegates, all of whom are recallable, limited-term, and drawn from the grassroots. For a specified period this group makes up the core administration, with a clear and limited mandate to make uncontroversial but necessary day-to-day metabolic decisions. For decisions affecting future-orientation such as realigning the ecology's short-, medium- and long-term goals, these must go to the wider membership. This ensures a balance between the quick decision making of the committee (sharpened sensing), the accountability of democratic election (adaptability of the sensing), while preventing the creation of a leadership clique (utilizing the strength of weak ties, avoiding the creation of vital organs), and spreading the empowerment of leadership to a wider pool of people. It has the advantages of a temporary 'vanguard' but avoids the rigidity and lack of unaccountability this usually brings.

With this Story, Strategy and Structure clarified, presented accessibly and delivered in an emotionally engaging way, we can provide a clear entry point for the newly mobilized, overcoming the impenetrable and isolated culture of left organizing, with actions to take quickly, and a means of directing people to existing groups. The ecology becomes a sort of town in which we act as tour guides, introducing people to the sights. Mapping this landscape for the benefit of new recruits is a vital task of the ecology, as is mapping the interests, skills and capacity of people and groups so that power can be better distributed.

Accelerating Action

Shocks provide the impetus for the ecology's growth. The necessity of orienting around external shocks has already been commented on – through escalating direct action and a readiness for social crises. But controlled *internal* shocks can also accelerate organizational processes.

When we create short-term, measurable and winnable goals, we create a fork in the path. You either succeed or fail, and the tension between these two and the alternative futures they open up stirs mobilization. We have seen this already in elections, particularly in the UK snap election of 2017, which along with the existing infrastructure of Momentum created an unprecedented turnaround in public opinion in only seven weeks. Clear short-term goals polarize, unify action and solidify collective identity.

By integrating a mechanism into the ecology for drawing up collectively agreed short-term goals, this same mobilizing capacity can be used for organizational speed. For example, the internal democratic process could include at regular intervals a vote on what the next periodic goal/s should be. Regular reports on the internal and external situation would inform decision making, including successes and failures of various subgroups and parts of the ecology, where there was a surplus or deficit of resources, important wider political context and so on. From this, the assembly chooses through one or more winnable short-term goals.

The wide support and democratic process helps to ensure members have a sense of urgency, excitement and empowerment. Both initiating and winning goals creates regular internal shocks that maintain pace. Autonomous groups would be created to press forward with projects, formed of people from across the ecology and mandated for the period of the goal to take certain actions. Reporting on what was learned and embedding that in the structure of the ecology helps it to adapt. And by dissolving these project groups on completion we avoid the encroaching rigidity, inaccessibility and unaccountability of path dependence.

The Care Ethic

Work is the source of oppression most widely shared by human beings. As the best potential site of common ground it absolutely must play a core role in a revolutionary movement. But given the initial conditions of our struggle will guide its direction, we cannot simply accept the concept of work as it currently exists, with its implications of an oppressive capitalist work ethic. We must struggle to redefine work.

The Care Ethic recognizes the 'work' that people perform simply in order to survive, and how this is at present unevenly distributed. It recognizes that work is not inherently valuable, but only by virtue of the role it can play in building a resilient new world, and fighting against the current one. The Care Ethic requires that we are always open to the complexities of bodies, seeking to understand people, organizations, communities and so on in all their parts and wholes, pasts, presents and futures.

The Care Ethic applied to movement bodies means recognizing our embodied needs, whether friendship, fun, relaxation, the joy of victory, or a shoulder to cry on. It means being alive to the uniqueness and differentiation of bodies: the varying experiences of traumas, oppressions, positions of power, of varying hopes and desires and fears. The Care Ethic means supporting people to articulate their stories; it means recognizing the capacity to make mistakes and to grow from them; and it compels us to empower others from the moment they enter the room.

On a wider level, the Care Ethic translates into a world where caring roles (of children, the sick, disabled and elderly) are accorded far greater value, and the responsibilities shared more evenly. It entails a world in which the work we do is empowering and not soul crushing, where choice replaces coercion. A world where we are not limited by rigid pre-existing spheres – the nuclear family, the workplace, the school – but where everything is opened up to redesign, to better accommodate the diversity of needs and desires. And as is crucial to our survival as a species, it is a world where the present goals of endless growth, personal enrichment and national rivalry are replaced with care for the earth as a whole.

Autonomy-Supporting Reforms

However different parts of the left choose to interact with the state, there should be one thing upon which we can agree: any action by the state is most to our advantage if it expands the capacity of social movements to organize. We must avoid close coupling of the ecology to the state, but maintain room for those who do engage with it, such as NGOs, charities and so on. The question is always whether any action leads to an increase in autonomy and power.

While different reforms could be argued for within the same model, I would advocate proposals such as:

- lowering the working week (giving more time and energy to organize);
- decriminalizing squatting (providing spaces in which to organize);

- decriminalizing solidarity strikes (allowing greater popular power);
- supporting workers to take over businesses and state-run services (expanding autonomy beyond state and capital);
- introducing a universal basic income (expanded autonomy from need to work);
- the 'universal basic services' proposal to extend free public services into food, transport, internet and housing (supporting individual and organizational metabolisms).

Whatever reforms are chosen in a particular context, the extent to which a reform is reversible is key. This is implied by 'autonomy supporting reforms'; if a reform is easily reversible, then any gains can be easily taken back, and so any autonomy provided is to some extent an illusion. This is not to say that we cannot or should not campaign for certain reversible reforms, as they can be extremely powerful. This principle simply says that, while we may disagree on whether a reversible reform is an effective way to achieve change, we come together at the least around autonomy-supporting reforms, just as many parts of the left came together historically to fight for the eight-hour day.

With both coherence of individual actions, and cohesion in shared principles, we now have a movement body, empowered, able to act as one. So, what should it do? How does it ultimately crush capitalism?

I present an idealized path below. Make of it what you will; stating it at least provides an image to react against, critique, test and adapt. The guiding force of future visions has been restated throughout this book. These are only 'utopian' in the negative sense when they remain a fantasy that has no effect on action. When it is a horizon that draws us towards it, such visions are indispensable.

The Path and the Future

Our ecology, growing in size and strength, is both attacking the current system and creating a viable alternative to it. Its growth is not only geographically contiguous, but networks with other urban areas, creating a larger nested body of bodies, stretching globally. Just as organizations were created to seed neoliberal think tanks across the world, our ecology has modules which aim to do the same, cooperating with global movements to construct and spread shared DNA. The guided self-organization approach is enabling sustainable worldwide viral growth, while allowing new ecologies to adapt to local conditions and be led by those on the ground.

As capacity grows, we become able to perform larger and longer-term disruptive actions to take parts of the capitalist system out of action. Small disruptions escalate in size and link together, finding and creating common ground between struggles, stabilized by the shared future vision. Individual workplace strikes become whole communities, whole cities on strike, to transnational social strikes coordinated across vast distances. Each wave disables more capitalist bodies, mobilizes more people, and entrenches our alternatives.

These alternatives, including an autonomous democratic system, create a tension with the state during this period. The techniques of self-organization that the ecology is constantly seeding into communities and workplaces is rebuilding sustainable popular power. Militant direct action is forcing concessions on democratic ownership and control from below, and new cooperative bodies are being created rapidly. As new powers emerge in the ecology, so does the legitimacy of disrupting existing capitalist models to replace with our own. This extends beyond traditional worker control of industry, applying the care ethic to new models of family, education, community healthcare and justice.

The movement is now looking towards its own future, and the possibility of the end of the state itself. The knowledge of chaos and complexity now broadly held in the movement leads to certain guiding conclusions about the state:

Firstly, that the state – and indeed all dominating bodies – will not wither away of its own accord. Further, for it to be toppled will require an escalating but controlled cascade of collapses, rather than a single revolutionary moment. As well as the accelerating movement outside the state, parts of the state should be progressively disempowered from within, such as state-owned utilities turned to common ownership and control, devolution of democratic powers, and massive criminal justice reform.

Secondly, should we succeed, this will not be the end of the matter. There must be cultural and institutional mechanisms in place to ward off the re-emergence of such dominating bodies, of endless growth and accumulation, and fossilized inequalities of class, race, gender or disability. This cannot involve the state repressing the people, however, but the converse: the people repressing the re-emergence of the state and other bodies of domination. This must come both through symbolic Care Ethic practices embedded in common sense, and through formal institutional processes carried out by the ecology to maintain grassroots power.

So there we have it: the Shock Doctrine of the Left. After all that theory, allow me to end on a practical note, an attempt at empowering a final few bodies – a call to arms if you will. Theory is nothing without its application, so if anything in this book made you think 'yes!', whether the whole work or just one solitary idea: try it. Fail, evaluate, adapt. The body of our social movement will only evolve through those kinds of interventions, by you. If you are an experienced organizer, I hope there is something in this book that helps you. If you have never taken any political action, I hope this book inspires you to begin.

The world is a body. You are a body. And every body is an organizer. So, organize!

Further Reading

The Catalan Integral Cooperative: An Organizational Study of a Post-Capitalist Cooperative by George Dafermos (available at https://p2pfounda

tion.net) is a detailed study of a successful modern solidarity economy project. *Accelerate* by John Kotter, although aimed at business management, contains relevant ideas for organizational speed and adaptation, and blending horizontal and hierarchical forms. Transnational Social Strike Platform (https://www.transnational-strike.info/) is building the cross-border actions necessary to our strategy. *Xenofeminism* by Helen Hester moves accelerationist discussions forward with a focus on queer feminist visions of intimate social and family relations. *Building the Commune: Radical Democracy in Venezuela* by George Ciccariello-Maher shows a contemporary attempt to build wide-scale political autonomy, mirroring some aspects of our strategy, while demonstrating how local context and events will inevitably take movements in different directions. And finally *Inventing the Future: Postcapitalism and a World Without Work* by Nick Srnicek and Alex Williams, which sparked the recent move towards strategic and utopian thinking, a conversation which I hope this book has contributed to.

Bibliography

Alexander, J. C. (2012) *Trauma: A Social Theory*. Polity.

Anarchist Federation (2014) *The Role of the Revolutionary Organization*.

Anderson, B. (1983) *Imagined Communities*. Verso.

ANON (2017) #AltWoke Manifesto.

Arendt, H. (1998) *The Human Condition*. University of Chicago Press.

Arrighi, G., Hopkins, T. and Wallerstein, I. M. (2012) *Anti-Systemic Movements*. Verso.

Barabási, A.-L. (2002) *Linked: The New Science of Networks*. Perseus Publishing.

___ (2016) *Network Science*. Cambridge University Press.

Bateson, G. (1972) *Steps to an Ecology of Mind. Collected Essays in Anthropology, Psychiatry, Evolution, and Epistemology*. Jason Aronson Inc.

Bauman, Z. (2003) *Wasted Lives: Modernity and its Outcasts*. Polity.

Beer, S. (1974) *Designing Freedom*. John Wiley & Sons Ltd.

Berila, B. (2016) *Integrating Mindfulness into Anti-Oppression Pedagogy: Social Justice in Higher Education*. Routledge.

Bhaskar, R. (1979) *The Possibility of Naturalism: A*

Bibliography

Philosophical Critique of the Contemporary Human Sciences. Harvester Press Ltd.

Birch, C. and Cobb Jr, J. B. (1981) *The Liberation of Life: From the Cell to the Community*. Cambridge University Press.

Bobo, K. (2001) *Organizing for Social Change: Midwest Academy Manual for Activists*. Midwest Academy.

Bogdanov, A. (1980) *Essays in Tektology: The General Science of Organization*. Intersystems Publications.

Bookchin, M. (2015) *The Next Revolution: Popular Assemblies and the Promise of Direct Democracy*. Verso.

Braidottti, R. (2013) *The Posthuman*. Polity.

Bratton, B. (2014) 'The Black Stack', *E-Flux*, 53.

___ (2016) *The Stack: On Software and Sovereignty*. MIT Press.

Bray, M. (2014) 'Five Liberal Tendencies that Plagued Occupy', *ROAR*.

Bryant, L. R. (2011) *The Democracy of Objects*. Open Humanities Press.

Buchanan, I. M. (2008) *Deleuze and Guattari's Anti-Oedipus: A Reader's Guide*. Continuum.

Burt, R. S. (1995) *Structural Holes: The Social Structure of Competition*. Harvard University Press.

Byrne, D. (1998) *Complexity Theory and the Social Sciences: An Introduction*. Routledge.

Caffentzis, G. (2013) *In Letters of Blood and Fire: Work, Machines, and the Crisis of Capitalism*. PM Press.

Capra, F. and Luisi, P. L. (2014) *The Systems View of Life: A Unifying Vision*. Cambridge University Press.

Castells, M. (2009) *Communication Power*. Oxford University Press.

___ (2011) 'A Network Theory of Power', *International Journal of Communication*, 5 (1).

___ (2012) *Networks of Outrage and Hope: Social Movements in the Internet Age*. Polity.

Chenoweth, E. and Stephan, M. (2011) *Why Civil Resistance*

Bibliography

Works: The Strategic Logic of Nonviolent Conflict. Columbia University Press.

Chesters, G. and Welsh, I. (2006) *Complexity and Social Movements: Multitudes at the Edge of Chaos.* Routledge.

Ciccariello-Maher, G. (2016) *Building the Commune.* Verso.

Clark, A. (2008) *Supersizing the Mind: Embodiment, Action, and Cognitive Extension.* Oxford University Press.

Clarke, S. and Campbell, C. (2015) 'Beyond the Right/Wrong Trap: Transforming Conflict into Creativity'. [Online Video].

Clastres, P. (1989) *Society Against the State: Essays in Political Anthropology.* Zone Books.

Coleman, M. A. (2008) *Making a Way Out of No Way: A Womanist Theology.* Fortress Press.

Collins, P. H. (2008) *Black Feminist Thought: Knowledge, Consciousness, and the Politics of Empowerment.* Routledge.

Connolly, W. E. (2014) 'Freedom, Teleodynamism, Creativity', *Foucault Studies* (17).

D'Alisa, G., Demaria, F. and Kallis, G. (2015) *Degrowth: A Vocabulary for a New Era.* Routledge.

Damasio, A. (2004) *Looking for Spinoza: Joy, Sorrow, and the Feeling Brain.* Vintage.

Davis, G. F. et al. (2005) *Social Movements and Organization Theory.* Cambridge University Press.

Davis, J. et al. (2014) *Scaling Up the Cooperative Movement: a Grassroots Economic Organizing Ebook.* The Democracy Collaborative.

Deacon, T. W. (2011) *Incomplete Nature: How Mind Emerged from Matter.* W. W. Norton & Company.

DeLanda, M. (2002) *Intensive Science and Virtual Philosophy.* Continuum.

___ (2006) *A New Philosophy of Society: Assemblage Theory and Social Complexity.* Continuum.

Deleuze, G. and Guattari, F. (1983) *Anti-Oedipus: Capitalism and Schizophrenia.* University of Minnesota Press.

Bibliography

___ (2004) *A Thousand Plateaus: Capitalism and Schizophrenia*. Continuum.

Durand, R. (2014) *Organizations, Strategy and Society: The Orgology of Disorganized Worlds*. Routledge.

Engels, F. (1987) *Anti-Duhring and Dialectics of Nature*. Lawrence & Wishart.

Engler, M. and Engler, P. (2016) *This is an Uprising: How Nonviolent Revolt is Shaping the Twenty-First Century*. Nation Books.

Federici, S. (2012) *Revolution at Point Zero: Housework, Reproduction and Feminist Struggle*. PM Press.

Fisher, M. (2009) *Capitalist Realism: Is There No Alternative?* Zero Books.

Foster, J. B. (2000) *Marx's Ecology: Materialism and Nature*. Monthly Review Press.

Francisco, V., Thompson, E. and Rosch, E. (1993) *The Embodied Mind: Cognitive Science and Human Experience*. MIT Press.

Frase, P. (2012) *Four Futures*. Jacobin.

Freire, P. (2005) *Pedagogy of the Oppressed*. Continuum.

Gallagher, S. and Zahavi, D. (2012) *The Phenomenological Mind*. Routledge.

Gee, T. (2011) *Counterpower: Making Change Happen*. New Internationalist Publications.

Gibson-Graham, J. K. (2006) *A Postcapitalist Politics*. Minnesota Press.

Gilbert, J. (2014) *Common Ground: Democracy and Collectivity in an Age of Individualism*. Pluto.

Goerner, S. (2017) 'The Science of Flow Says Extreme Inequality Causes Economic Collapse', *Evonomics*.

Gotts, N. M. (2007) 'Resilience, Panarchy, and World-Systems Analysis', *Ecology and Society*, 12(1).

Graeber, D. (2013) 'On the Phenomenon of Bullshit Jobs', *Strike Mag.*

Graham, S. (2010) *Disrupted Cities: When Infrastructure Fails*. Routledge.

Bibliography

Guanyem Barcelona (2015) 'Handy Guide to Setting Up a Guanyem', http://www.manuelbompard.fr/wp-content/uploads/2015/05/handy-guide.pdf.

Gunderson, L. H. and Holling, C. S. (2002) *Panarchy: Understanding Transformations in Human and Natural Systems*. Island Press.

Hahnel, R. and Wright, E. O. (2014) *Alternatives to Capitalism: Proposals for a Democratic Economy*. New Left Project.

Hallam, R. (2016) *How to Win: Successful Procedures and Mechanisms for Radical Campaign Groups*. Radical Think Tank.

Harvey, D. (2012) *Rebel Cities: From the Right to the City to the Urban Revolution*. Verso.

Hassan, B. (2015) 'Radical Lives: Omar Aziz'. *Novara*.

Holland, E. W. (1999) *Deleuze and Guattari's Anti-Oedipus: Introduction to Schizoanalysis*. Routledge.

Hutchins, E. (1995) *Cognition in the Wild*. MIT Press.

Jessop, B. (2001) 'State Theory, Regulation, and Autopoiesis: Debates and Controversies', *Capital and Class*, 25(3).

___ (2002) *The Future of the Capitalist State*. Polity.

Juarrero, A. (2002) *Dynamics in Action: Intentional Behaviour as a Complex System*. MIT Press.

Kallis, G. and Vansintjan, A. (ed) (2017) *In Defense of Degrowth: Opinions and Minifestos*.

Klein, N. (2011) *The Shock Doctrine: The Rise of Disaster Capitalism*. Metropolitan Books.

___ (2017) *No is not Enough: Defeating the New Shock Politics*. Allen Lane.

Knott, E. (2014) *Rules without Rulers: The Possibilities and Limits of Anarchism*. Zero Books.

Koebler, J. (2016) 'Society is Too Complex to Have a President, Complex Mathematics Suggest', *Vice*.

Kotter, J. P. (2012) 'Accelerate!', *Harvard Business Review*.

___ (2014) *Accelerate: Building Strategic Agility for a Faster Moving World*. Harvard Business Review Press.

Bibliography

Laboria Cuboniks (2016) Manifesto on Xenofeminism: A Politics for Alienation. *e-flux*.

Laclau, E. (2005) *On Populist Reason*. Verso.

Lakoff, G. (1987) *Women, Fire and Dangerous Things: What Categories Reveal About the Mind*. University of Chicago Press.

Latour, B. (2005) *Reassembling the Social: An Introduction to Actor-Network-Theory*. Oxford University Press.

Levin, S. (1999) *Fragile Dominion: Complexity and the Commons*. Helix Books.

Liacas, T. and Mogus, J. (2017) 'Networked Change in Canada', *Broadbent Institute*.

Libcom (2011) *Building a Solidarity Network Guide*.

Lorde, A. (1984) *Sister Outsider*. Crossing Press.

Luhmann, N. (2013) *Introduction to Systems Theory*. Polity.

Mackay, R. and Avanessian, A. (eds.) (2014) *Accelerate: The Accelerationist Reader*. Urbanomic.

Mason, P. (2016) *Postcapitalism: A Guide to Our Future*. Penguin.

Maturana, H. R. and Varela, F. J. (1992) *The Tree of Knowledge: The Biological Roots of Human Understanding*. Shambhala Publications.

McAdam, D., Tarrow, S. and Tilly, C. (2004) *Dynamics of Contention*. Cambridge University Press.

McAlevey, J. F. (2016) *No Shortcuts: Organizing for Power in the New Gilded Age*. Oxford University Press.

Medhurst, J. (2017) *No Less Than Mystic: A History of Lenin and the Russian Revolution for a 21st-Century Left*. Repeater Books.

Mesle, C. R. (2008) *Process-Relational Philosophy: An Introduction to Alfred North Whitehead*. Templeton Foundation Press.

Milburn, K. (2015) 'On Social Strikes and Directional Demands', *Plan C*.

Miller, E. (2006) 'Other Economies are Possible: Building a Solidarity Economy', *Grassroots Economic Organising*.

Bibliography

Murray, A. and German, L. (2005) *Stop the War: The Story of Britain's Biggest Mass Movement*. Bookmarks.

Nail, T. (2012) *Returning to Revolution: Deleuze, Guattari and Zapatismo*. Edinburgh University Press.

Noys, B. (2012) *Communization and its Discontents: Contestation, Critique, and Contemporary Struggles*. Minor Compositions.

Nunes, R. (2014) *Organization of the Organizationless: Collective Action After Networks*. PML Books.

Ostrom, E. (1990) *Governing the Commons: The Evolution of Institutions for Collective Action*. Cambridge University Press.

Out of the Woods (2014) 'Disaster Communism', *The Occupied Times*.

Padgett, J. F. and Powell, W. W. (2012) *The Emergence of Organizations and Markets*. Princeton University Press.

Panksepp, J. (1998) *Affective Neuroscience: The Foundations of Human and Animal Emotions*. Oxford University Press.

Pomeroy, A. F. (2004) *Marx and Whitehead: Process, Dialectics, and the Critique of Capitalism*. State University of New York Press.

Poulantzas, N. (2014) *State, Power, Socialism*. Verso.

Prigogine, I. and Stengers, I. (1984) *Order Out of Chaos*. Bantam Books.

Prokopenko, M. (ed) (2014) *Guided Self-Organization: Inception*. Springer.

Protevi, J. (2009) *Political Affect: Connecting the Social and the Somatic*. University of Minnesota Press.

Robert McConnell Productions (2001) *Robert's Rules of Order: Simplified and Applied*. Wiley.

Saavedra, C., Engler, P. and Rodriguez, B. (2014) 'Momentum Webinar 2: The Theory of Integration'. [Online Video].

Sampson, T. D. (2012) *Virality: Contagion Theory in the Age of Networks*. University of Minnesota Press.

Bibliography

Sassen, S. (2014) *Expulsions: Brutality and Complexity in the Global Economy.* Harvard University Press.

Schneider, N. (2015) 'On the Lam with Bank Robber Enric Duran'. *Vice.*

Schulman, S. (2017) *Conflict is Not Abuse: Overstating Harm, Community Responsibility and the Duty of Repair.* Arsenal Pulp Press.

Scott, J. C. (1998) *Seeing Like a State: How Certain Schemes to Improve the Human Condition Have Failed.* Yale University Press.

Shalom, S. and Doherty, A. (2010) 'The Politics of a Good Society', *New Left Project.*

Sharifian, F. (2011) *Cultural Conceptualisations and Language.* John Benjamins.

Sharp, G. (1990) *Civilian-Based Defense: A Post-Military Weapons System.* Princeton University Press.

Sharp, G. and Jenkins, B. (2003) *The Anti-Coup.* Albert Einstein Institution.

Smucker, J. (2017) *Hegemony How-To: A Roadmap for Radicals.* AK Press.

Srnicek, N. (2007) *Assemblage Theory, Complexity and Contentious Politics: The Political Ontology of Gilles Deleuze.* University of Western Ontario.

Srnicek, N. and Williams, A. (2015) *Inventing the Future: Postcapitalism and a World Without Work.* Verso.

Stanford, N. (2015) *The Economist Guide to Organization Design: Creating High-Performing and Adaptable Enterprises.* Profile Books.

Strogatz, S. (2003) *Sync: How Order Emerges from Chaos in the Universe, Nature and Daily Life.* Hyperion.

Swann, T. (2014) 'The Cybernetics of Occupy: An Anarchist Perspective', *ROAR.*

Tainter, J. A. (1988) *The Collapse of Complex Societies.* Cambridge University Press.

Thibault, P. (2004) *Brain, Mind and the Signifying Body: An Ecosocial Semiotic Theory.* Continuum.

Bibliography

Thompson, E. (2007) *Mind in Life: Biology, Phenomenology and the Sciences of Mind*. Harvard University Press.

van der Kolk, B. (2015) *The Body Keeps the Score: Brain, Mind, and Body in the Healing of Trauma*. Penguin.

Vansintjan, A. (2016) 'Accelerationism . . . and Degrowth? The Left's Strange Bedfellows', *Institute for Social Ecology*.

Varela, F. (1999) *Ethical Know-How: Action, Wisdom, and Cognition*. Stanford University Press.

Vitale, C. (2014) *Networkologies: A Philosophy of Networks for a Hyperconnected Age – A Manifesto*. Zero Books.

Wacquant, L. (2011) 'The Punitive Regulation of Poverty in the Neoliberal Age'. *OpenDemocracy*.

Walby, S. (2007) 'Complexity Theory, Systems Theory, and Multiple Intersecting Social Inequalities', *Philosophy of the Social Sciences*, 37.

Walker, B. and Salt, D. (2006) *Resilience Thinking: Sustaining Ecosystems and People in a Changing World*. Island Press.

___ (2012) *Resilience Practice: Building Capacity to Absorb Disturbance and Maintain Function*. Island Press.

Wark, M. (2015) *Molecular Red: Theory for the Anthropocene*. Verso.

Wasdell, D. (2012) 'Catastrophic Climate Change and Runaway Global Warming'. [Online Video].

Weeks, K. (2011) *The Problem with Work: Feminism, Marxism, Antiwork Politics, and Postwork Imaginaries*. Duke University Press.

Whitehead, A. N. (1978) *Process and Reality: An Essay in Cosmology*. The Free Press.

Williams, A. (2015) *Complexity and Hegemony*. University of East London.

Wright, E. O. (2010) *Envisioning Real Utopias*. Verso.

___ (2015) *How to Be an Anticapitalist Today*. Jacobin.

Young, I. M. (2003) 'Five Faces of Oppression', in Heldke, L. and O'Connor, P. (eds.) *Oppression, Privilege, and Resistance: Theoretical Perspectives on Racism, Sexism and Heterosexism*. McGraw-Hill.